Is Jesus Real?

A Journal Bible Study Exploring the Evidence with the Book of Luke

Sandy K. Cook

Published by Psalm 30 Publishing,
© 2019 Sandra K. Cook, All rights reserved.

Cover Photo credit: https://www.pexels.com/@felixmittermeier, "Silhouette of Person Under Blue and Purple Sky," used under Free to use, public domain open license, with no attribution required.

ISBN: 978-1-948953-05-4

The contents of this book are protected by U.S. Copyright laws. No part of this book may be copied electronically, by photocopy, reproduced in digital format, or distributed by any means whatsoever without explicit written permission from Psalm 30 Publishing. Requests for permissions may be addressed to:

Psalm 30 Publishing
P.O. Box 491328
Lawrenceville, GA 30049

Unless otherwise noted, Bible verses printed in this book are taken from translations of the Bible that are in the Public Domain. Verses have been taken from an ASV-based, Public Domain translation, and have been modified to revert back from the use of the formal name of God, which was added in that translation. Within this book, God is addressed as God, The Lord, or Jesus throughout the book. As required by the Public Domain permissions of the secondary Public Domain source, the specific secondary Public Domain source will remain unidentified in this publication, because some verses have been modified and no longer directly reflect the content of the specific public domain source.

Table of Contents

A LOOK BEFORE YOU LEAP 1
CHAPTER 1 7
CHAPTER 2 17
CHAPTER 3 25
CHAPTER 4 31
CHAPTER 5 39
CHAPTER 6 45
CHAPTER 7 53
CHAPTER 8 59
CHAPTER 9 67
CHAPTER 10 75
CHAPTER 11 81
CHAPTER 12 89
CHAPTER 13 97
CHAPTER 14 103
CHAPTER 15 109
CHAPTER 16 113
CHAPTER 17 119
CHAPTER 18 125
CHAPTER 19 131
CHAPTER 20 137
CHAPTER 21 143
CHAPTER 22 149
CHAPTER 23 157
CHAPTER 24 165
BONUS CHAPTER: Chapter 1 ~ ACTS OF THE APOSTLES.......................171
CONCLUSION 177
REFERENCE LINKS...181
ABOUT THE AUTHOR 189
OTHER BOOKS BY SANDY K. COOK 191

A LOOK BEFORE YOU LEAP

How Can We Know If Jesus Is REAL?

One thing we know: Jesus is either real or He isn't. If He is real, we then need to decide what we believe is true about Him; if He isn't real, then nothing else matters.

Let me start by saying this is not going to be your typical "Jesus is Real" book. The fact is, there are atheistic scientists in academia who say Biblical Archaeology is faked, there is no proof, etc. Those who are adamantly against the Bible consistently hold narratives the Bible is completely fictional, even when there is evidence otherwise. On the flip-side, those who are passionate about the Bible may trumpet every new discovery as proof positive everything in the Bible is factual. How can you know what's true? How can you figure out the facts?

In this book, we're going to take a look at evidence related to the people, places and practices mentioned in the Bible. I'll let you decide whether you think the body of evidence points to the factual or false nature of what the Bible says about Jesus.

The field of Biblical archaeology has qualified, degreed archaeologists, the Biblical Archaeology Review, and other publications. They provide verifiable evidence. There are carbon dated artifacts, DNA analyzed bone fragments, and validated documents. Many items point to the historical truth in the Bible, but some facts have not been confirmed. Ultimately, you will have to decide the truth for yourself after considering the available evidence.

In other words, if you are searching for evidence one way or the other, looking at the archaeology and documentation is a wise choice. Since there are opposing opinions on many archaeological finds related to the Bible, you won't be able to rely solely on what someone else tells you. You can rely on facts about long-preserved artifacts and what we know from historical documents within and outside of the Bible.

Therefore, our approach in this Journal Bible Study is going to be one of looking at facts presented in the Bible as they relate to tangible evidence we have available. We will look at the biblical narratives, related artifacts, and historical documents. We'll use logic and reasoning to determine what we think is likely to be true.

In other words, I'm not going to tell you what to think about the evidence we have, but I will present the archaeology, historical documents, and ways of thinking for your consideration and analysis. The end of chapter questions will reflect the process I went through as I searched and weighed options in order to decide the truth for myself.

Some general questions for you to ponder before starting this study:

- What might cause ancient people to divide the world's timeline into the eras of B.C. (Before Christ) and A.D. (Anno Domini [Year of our Lord]), if Jesus was an ordinary man or wasn't real at all?
- The historians and official records for Judaism, Islam (Quran), and Christianity (Bible) ALL acknowledge Jesus as a real, living person in the first century. They differ in their judgement about who Jesus was. Why do these three leading religions acknowledge Jesus was a wise man and a great prophet, yet two of the three think Jesus blatantly lied about who He is?
- How could 40 authors, writing independent books over a span of 1,500 years, accurately prophecy and write a cohesive manuscript about Jesus, which suddenly fooled millions of people in the 1st century A.D. into believing Jesus was a real person?
- Why would multiple independent authors write about a man named Jesus, providing timeless, godly wisdom and truth for living, give credit to Jesus, and then be martyred, rather than recant?

When it comes to these questions, use your own reasoning and logic, along with the history of the world, archaeological finds, the biblical narrative, and your knowledge of typical human behavior to determine for yourself whether you think Jesus is real.

If you decide Jesus is real, then you have to decide WHAT you believe about Jesus. Was he "just a man?" Is he the Son of God? Is Jesus the Savior of the World?

Additionally, as you move forward, keep in mind the basic concept: "Absence of evidence isn't evidence of absence" (i.1). In other words, there may be evidence we simply haven't found yet. This has been the case for several former beliefs against the Bible's factual nature, which is increasingly proven through archaeological finds which verify the existence of ancient cities and practices.

We will be basing our study on the Book of Luke, because it is known to be the most historically detailed and accurate of the four Gospel narratives in the Bible.

Think of Luke as a modern-day investigative reporter. He was a physician by trade. Luke was an intelligent man interested in gathering facts about Jesus. His book was written around 60 AD or earlier. So, it was written within 30 years of Jesus's death, when many eye-witnesses were still living.

We will assume Luke's account is an investigative, journalistic report, seeking out the facts and reporting, just like historians of any era. If we regard Luke's book as an account of events of the time, we can use it as a roadmap for verifying the things that are written about Jesus. Luke's account can be held in the same regard as Taciticus's, Polybius's, and other ancient historical writers's accounts.

It's also worth noting, Sir William Ramsay researched in an attempt to prove the book of Luke is false, but after researching he concluded, "Luke is a historian of the first rank." Luke documented details with names and places, which we can use to investigate what other sources say about Jesus.

The one assumption I will be making in the questions I've written for this book is that you, the reader, at a minimum believe in the possibility of a spiritual realm. I'm telling you this up front, so you won't necessarily think I am trying to sell you on the fact that there is a spiritual realm. This is important because a person's beliefs about Jesus as potentially the son of God, will be grounded in their personal belief about whether there is a God and a spiritual realm.

Therefore, in each chapter, you will encounter of a variety of questions. Some will be prime questions you should ask yourself when you're considering what you believe. Others will be life application questions, which are presented for to you reflect on how your beliefs about the events described in the Book of Luke apply to your life. The majority of questions will be reflective thinking questions allowing you to weigh the evidence's factual nature against what Luke writes. Reflecting on the evidence and questions will help shape your beliefs based on the information presented.

In any chapter, feel free to embark on additional Research of your own. There is an appendix in the back, which contains reference notes for each chapter. You can visit any of the sites where the information for this study was obtained and read the full articles. In many cases, several resources were researched, but the one relied on most heavily will be the one referenced.

While this book is not entirely free of persuasive language, I have tried to keep my opinion to a minimum to allow you to process the information and make a decision for yourself.

I hope this journal Bible study is helpful to you, and leads you to a greater confidence in your personal beliefs, whatever they end up being!

What Kind of Bible Study is This?

This is an open-ended, reflective, and life-application study. It's a combination book, journal, and workbook. The study is open-ended and reflective, because it is designed to let God show you what He wants YOU to see. Many of the questions will explore how God's Word applies to your individual life. That is the life-application aspect of the study.

In this study, you are encouraged to pray and ask God for insight into His word, as it applies to you and your life. What you get out of each chapter will be between you and God. Your takeaways will depend upon your life circumstances, as well as how purposefully you seek to understand God's Word.

If you are in a Bible study group, discussing each person's insights can be eye-opening. Everyone gains different insights from a study like this, because everyone's life experiences are different.

If you don't belong to a Bible study group, feel free to use resources, like Bible commentaries, to learn more. You can also gain understanding by rereading the texts and praying. God made the Bible to be understood by common people, so everyone can gain a measure of personal insight from this study.

Lastly, this is a God-directed Bible study. In other words, as you read, pray and ask God for insight. Ask Him to show you the things He wants you to see. God will bring to your mind ideas and truths that are personally meaningful to you.

How To Use This Journal Bible Study

In this Journal Bible Study, each chapter covers one chapter in the Book of Luke. There are no verse numbers, since Luke originally wrote his story as a book without numbered verses. Removing verse numbers will let your reading flow smoothly, as the book was originally intended to be read.

Next to each column of story text, there is a wide margin for your note taking or journaling. The margin is designed for you to write down anything that comes to your mind as you read. You can use the journal area to make notes about:

- Questions you have,
- Your emotions and reactions,
- Your thoughts about Jesus' teachings and actions,
- Your reaction to Jesus' commands,
- How you feel the text relates to your life or your personal character,
- Or any thought which comes to mind while you're reading.

If you like to draw or color, the open space allows you to interact with the Bible text through your artistic expression. You can highlight, underline, draw arrows, and mark this book all up!

One of the main features of this Bible study is that all of the chapters of the Gospel of Luke are included. All you need is this book, a pen or pencil, and time to read and relate to God's Word.

Including the entire Book of Luke here serves two purposes:

1. It makes studying more convenient, because you won't have to go back-and-forth between a workbook, journal, and your Bible. You can read the text and answer the questions inside this workbook journal.
2. Including the full text makes this study simple for you. It can be difficult and time-consuming to locate passages in a Bible, especially if you're unfamiliar with the Bible's layout. Having to look up scriptures can also affect your ability to grasp the deeper meaning in verses.

By including the Bible text in this Journal, you can read continuously without stopping. Therefore, this Journal Bible Study is designed to be pain free—easy to use and easy to understand.

On a side note: even though this study includes the full Gospel of Luke, it's good for you to have an actual Bible to read too. The Psalm 30 Journal Bible Study series is designed to make studying individual books of the Bible easier by covering one book at a time. However, the entire Bible, taken as a whole, is critical for understanding God.

If you don't have your own Bible, and aren't sure how to choose a translation that is easy for you to read, visit: http://christianonlinebiblestudy.com/how-to-choose-a-bible/. That webpage shows you how to select a version which is easy for you to use. There are samples of different translations, so you can pick the one you like best. Finding a translation that is easy to read can make a big difference in your desire to read the Bible.

The best way to use this study is to settle in where you're comfortable and read a chapter. Before you begin reading, take a few minutes to pray. Praying is simply talking to God, as if He were a friend sitting next to you. Since God is Spirit, He is with us at all times wherever we go, and He will hear whatever you say or ask. You may want to pray something similar to this:

"Dear Lord, please open my mind and heart to understand whatever you want me to learn through this study today. Give me the knowledge and understanding I need. Please speak to my heart where I need to be touched. Help me see Jesus for who He truly is, and reveal Yourself to me. I ask these things in the name of Jesus, Amen."

As you read, interact with Luke's book by writing down your thoughts and reactions. Freely write whatever comes to your mind, highlight, et cetera. Reading actively will help you remember the details.

Explore how each chapter applies to your life, your actions, thoughts, and feelings. *Make this study personal. Make it about you and your relationship with God. Take time to think about what you're reading.*

Take the scriptures into your heart. Consider what the Bible verses mean to you personally.

Then thoughtfully answer each of the questions. Pause and reflect on the questions before answering them.

If you have no immediate reaction or thought about a question, pray over it. Ask God for His insight. Ask God to bring to your mind ideas about how the chapter and insights apply to you.

Quiet your spirit for a moment, and wait for meaningful insight to come into your mind. Take note of any thoughts the Holy Spirit brings to you.

Lastly, before diving into the study, let's see who Luke was.

Who was Luke?

From the mentions of Luke in the Bible, we know Luke was a physician. He was also a friend of Apostle Paul. We don't really know if Luke was a Gentile or Jewish, but he had a lot of knowledge about the Jewish scriptures, so we know he studied Jewish scriptures.

Luke was the author of both the Book of Luke and the Book of Acts. According to the Blue Letter Bible, "Not only did Luke compose the longest Gospel, but he also wrote more than any other New Testament writer" (i.2).

The Gospel of Luke's Authority

You might wonder when Luke's Book was written. The book of Luke has two primary dating factors:

1. Jerusalem has not yet been destroyed at the time Luke wrote his book. Therefore, we know Luke's book was written before 70 A.D.
2. The book of Luke and the book of Acts leave Apostle Paul in prison, so he was not yet martyred. From this we can deduce Luke's Gospel was written sometime in the late 50's A.D. or 60's A.D.

This means the book of Luke was written approximately 30 years after Jesus died.

There were still many people living who actually knew Jesus when the Gospel of Luke was written. Therefore, we can conclude Luke was able to interview eye-witnesses to learn their stories about what Jesus said, did, and the events in Jesus' life.

The four Gospel books (Matthew, Mark, Luke, and John) in the New Testament are all early, authentic documents referenced by other first century writers. All four of the New Testament Gospel books were written in the first century when people who actually knew Jesus were still alive.

We have more authenticated, preserved copies and evidence for the reliability of the four Gospels than we do for writings of Caesar, Plato, Aristotle, and other ancient authors. You can visit https://carm.org/manuscript-evidence to learn more about supporting evidence for the Bible's Gospels.

Whether you believe Jesus is real or not will depend heavily on whether you believe what Luke wrote about Jesus. It's no different than believing writings about Caesar, Plato, Aristotle and other great men in ancient history. Either the accounts are credible historical reports, or they are not. Only you can decide if you think the book of Luke is credible. With Luke's narrative, we also have supporting physical evidence for you to consider, just as we have for many other ancient historical figures.

Your final decision will also depend upon whether you pray for insight and understanding from God as you read, and the personal insights God gives you. As mentioned before, your decision also depends on how deep is your desire for a connection with God and your openness to learning whatever God wants you to learn.

In Matthew 7:7 Jesus tells us, "Ask, and it will be given you. Seek, and you will find. Knock, and it will be opened for you." So ASK God to help you see the truth in His Word anytime you don't understand something you've read.

Remember, praying to God is just like talking to a good friend sitting next to you, whether you speak aloud, or whether you just express yourself to God with words in your mind. At any point in your reading, you can stop and pray. Doing so will help you gain better understanding.

My hope in developing this Journal Bible Study is that you will be able to decide if Jesus is real, and that you will gain clarity in your own mind. I hope you are inspired by the Gospel message and find this is a worthwhile journey through the Book of Luke.

Are you ready to learn *Is Jesus Real*?

Let's dive into Luke's book and the evidence, so you can discover what God wants you to know..

CHAPTER 1

Since many have undertaken to set in order a narrative concerning those matters which have been fulfilled among us, even as those who from the beginning were eyewitnesses and servants of the word delivered them to us, it seemed good to me also, having traced the course of all things accurately from the first, to write to you in order, most excellent Theophilus; that you might know the certainty concerning the things in which you were instructed.

There was in the days of Herod, the king of Judea, a certain priest named Zacharias, of the priestly division of Abijah. He had a wife of the daughters of Aaron, and her name was Elizabeth. They were both righteous before God, walking blamelessly in all the commandments and ordinances of the Lord. But they had no child, because Elizabeth was barren, and they both were well advanced in years.

Now while he executed the priest's office before God in the order of his division according to the custom of the priest's office, his lot was to enter into the temple of the Lord and burn incense. The whole multitude of the people were praying outside at the hour of incense.

An angel of the Lord appeared to him, standing on the right side of the altar of incense. Zacharias was troubled when he saw him, and fear fell upon him. But the angel said to him, "Don't be afraid, Zacharias, because your request has been heard. Your wife, Elizabeth, will bear you a son, and you shall call his name John. You will have joy and gladness, and many will rejoice at his birth. For he will be great in the sight of the Lord, and he will drink no wine nor strong drink. He will be filled with the Holy Spirit, even from his mother's womb. He will turn many of the children of Israel to the Lord their God. He will go before him in the spirit and power of Elijah, 'to turn the hearts of the fathers to the children,' and the disobedient to the wisdom of the just; to prepare a people prepared for the Lord."

Zacharias said to the angel, "How can I be sure of this? For I am an old man, and my wife is well advanced in years."

The angel answered him, "I am Gabriel, who stands in the presence of God. I was sent to speak to you and to bring you this good news. Behold, you will be silent and not able to speak until the day that these things will happen, because you didn't believe my words, which will be fulfilled in their proper time."

The people were waiting for Zacharias, and they marveled that he delayed in the temple. When he came out, he could not speak to them. They perceived that he had seen a vision in the temple. He continued making signs to them, and remained mute. When the days of his service were fulfilled, he departed to his house. After these days Elizabeth his wife conceived, and she hid herself five months, saying, "Thus has the Lord done to me in the days in which he looked at me, to take away my reproach among men."

Now in the sixth month, the angel Gabriel was sent from God to a city of Galilee named Nazareth, to a virgin pledged to be married to a man whose name was Joseph, of David's house. The virgin's name was Mary. Having come in, the angel said to her, "Rejoice, you highly favored one! The Lord is with you. Blessed are you among women!"

But when she saw him, she was greatly troubled at the saying, and considered what kind of salutation this might be. The angel said to her, "Don't be afraid, Mary, for you have found favor with God. Behold, you will conceive in your womb and give birth to a son, and shall name him 'Jesus.' He will be great and will be called the Son of the Most High. The Lord God will give him the throne of his father David, and he will reign over the house of Jacob forever. There will be no end to his Kingdom."

Mary said to the angel, "How can this be, seeing I am a virgin?"

The angel answered her, "The Holy Spirit will come on you, and the power of the Most High will overshadow you. Therefore also the holy one who is born from you will be called the Son of God. Behold, Elizabeth your relative also has conceived a son in her old age; and this is the sixth month with her who was called barren. For nothing spoken by God is impossible."

Mary said, "Behold, the servant of the Lord; let it be done to me according to your word."

The angel departed from her.

Mary arose in those days and went into the hill country with haste, into a city of Judah, and entered into the house of Zacharias and greeted Elizabeth. When Elizabeth heard Mary's greeting, the baby leaped in her womb; and Elizabeth was filled with the Holy Spirit. She called out with a loud voice and said, "Blessed are you among women, and blessed is the fruit of your womb! Why am I so favored, that the mother of my Lord should come to me? For behold, when the voice of your greeting came into my ears, the baby leaped in my womb for joy! Blessed is she who believed, for there will be a fulfillment of the things which have been spoken to her from the Lord!"

Mary said, "My soul magnifies the Lord. My spirit has rejoiced in God my Savior, for he has looked at the humble state of his servant. For behold, from now on, all generations will call me blessed. For he who is mighty has done great things for me. Holy is his name. His mercy is for generations of generations on those who fear him. He has shown strength with his arm. He has scattered the proud in the imagination of their hearts. He has put down princes from their thrones, and has exalted the lowly. He has filled the hungry with good things. He has sent the rich away empty. He has given help to Israel, his servant, that he might remember mercy, as he spoke to our fathers, to Abraham and his offspring forever."

Mary stayed with her about three months, and then returned to her house.

Now the time that Elizabeth should give birth was fulfilled, and she gave birth to a son. Her neighbors and her relatives heard that the Lord had magnified his mercy toward her, and they rejoiced with her. On the eighth day, they came to circumcise the child; and they would have called him Zacharias, after the name of his father. His mother answered, "Not so; but he will be called John."

They said to her, "There is no one among your relatives who is called by this name." They made signs to his father, what he would have him called.

He asked for a writing tablet, and wrote, "His name is John."

They all marveled. His mouth was opened immediately and his tongue freed, and he spoke, blessing God. Fear came on all who lived around them, and all these sayings were talked about throughout all the hill country of Judea. All who heard them laid them up in their heart, saying, "What then will this child be?" The hand of the Lord was with him.

His father Zacharias was filled with the Holy Spirit, and prophesied, saying, "Blessed be the Lord, the God of Israel, for he has visited and redeemed his people; and has raised up a horn of salvation for us in the house of his servant David (as he spoke by the mouth of his holy prophets who have been from of old), salvation from our enemies and from the hand of all who hate us; to show mercy toward our fathers, to remember his holy covenant, the oath which he swore to Abraham our father, to grant to us that we, being delivered out of the hand of our enemies, should serve him without fear, in holiness and righteousness before him all the days of our life.

"And you, child, will be called a prophet of the Most High; for you will go before the face of the Lord to prepare his ways, to give knowledge of salvation to his people by the remission of their sins, because of the tender mercy of our God, by which the dawn from on high will visit us, to shine on those who sit in darkness and the shadow of death; to guide our feet into the way of peace."

The child was growing and becoming strong in spirit, and was in the desert until the day of his public appearance to Israel.

ARCHAEOLOGICAL AND HISTORICAL EVIDENCE:

Luke references a number of historical people and places. We have historical documents and artifacts to anchor Luke's account of Jesus's life to the real world. I will list the archaeology and historical documentation for people, places, and other factual information as we encounter them in this book.

You will find these early chapters have longer listings of evidence at the end of each chapter than the later chapters. Please don't let the length of the end of chapter information overwhelm you in these early chapters. The further we go into the book, the more we will already know about each person, place, and practice. Therefore, we won't have as much new material to cover at the end of later chapters.

Luke says he sought information from eyewitnesses and servants. Therefore, the events shared in Luke's Book are truthful to the extent any eyewitness's story is factual. While specific details might be left out, we know, overall, the stories are likely to be true as told by eyewitnesses.

Outside of what the Bible and Jewish scriptures tell us, we know little to nothing about Theophilus, Zacharias, Elizabeth, and Aaron, who are mentioned by Luke in this chapter. They were ordinary citizens, with no fame or notoriety at the time of Jesus's birth. Just like in your family history, your elders will remember family members and share stories about them, but the world at large preserves little to no archaeological evidence for their existence. When it comes to the story about Zacharias and Elizabeth, what we know is according to the accounts of eye witnesses, which are written here in Luke's book.

It's important to note there are two Herod's within Luke's account. Herod the Great ruled when Jesus was born. Herod Antipas, Herod the Great's son, was the ruler at the time of Jesus's crucifixion.

Herod Antipas was the son of Herod the Great. We know from historical documents, archaeology, coins and buildings, that Herod the Great was a real person. He founded cities and had coins minted in his likeness, according to BiblicalArchaeology.org and numerous other historical accounts.

"Herod the Great's reign over Judea from 37 to 4 B.C. is not remembered for justice, but for its indiscriminate cruelty. His most notorious act was the murder of all male infants in Bethlehem to prevent the fulfillment of a prophecy heralding the birth of the Messiah. There is no record of the decree other than the Gospel of Matthew, and biblical scholars debate whether it actually took place, but the story is in keeping with a man who arranged the murders of, among others, three of his own sons and a beloved wife" (1.2).

The "Herodium, also called Herodian, was first positively identified in 1838 by the American scholar Edward Robinson." (1.2) "In 1976, Netzer led a team that discovered the site of one of Herod's infamous misdeeds: the murder of his young brother-in-law, Aristobulus, whom Herod ordered to be drowned in a pool at his winter palace complex near Jericho" (1.2).

In 2007, The Tomb of Herod the Great was discovered at the Herodium by Ehud Netzer, a professor at the Hebrew University of Jerusalem Institute of Archaeology (1.3). Based on the excavations at the Herodian grounds, the discovery of Herod's tomb, and historical documentation, we know Herod the Great was a real person. His brutal manner of ruling is also documented and affirmed.

There is a large body of written history regarding Herod the Great, as well as numerous building projects he left behind. So much evidence exists, it would require an entire book to share all we know about Herod. If you'd like to know more, you can visit: https://www.britannica.com/biography/Herod-king-of-Judaea. Suffice it to say, no one really disputes whether King Herod was a real person. Since he was the king when and where Jesus lived, it makes sense that Herod the Great would be mentioned in the biography of Jesus's life.

Abijah, as mentioned in the lineage of Zacharias, has an archaeological find related to him. "In 1908 an exciting discovery was made at the site of the Biblical city of Gezer, which lies toward the coastal plain west of Jerusalem: a small limestone plaque, or tablet, believed to be from the tenth century B.C. On it, in ancient Hebrew script, was found what is thought to be a simplified version of an agricultural year, or cycle, with its various operations. This tablet has come to be known as the Gezer Calendar. The tablet bears a signature: Abijah" (1.6).

"The calendar (tablet) was dated to the middle 10th century B.C. - probably during Solomon's reign, when Gezer was under the control of the Israelites (1 Kings 9:16). To date, the Gezer Calendar is the earliest extant example of a Hebrew inscription and is an important piece of evidence" (1.7).

The events in Luke, Chapter 1 begin in the region of Judea, which still exists in the world today. "Geographers divide Judea into several regions: the Hebron hills, the Jerusalem saddle, the Bethel hills and the Judean desert east of Jerusalem, which descends in a series of steps to the Dead Sea. The hills are distinct for their anticline structure. In ancient times the hills were forested, and the Bible records agriculture and sheep farming being practiced in the area. Animals are still grazed today, with shepherds moving them between the low ground to the hilltops as summer approaches, while the slopes are still layered with centuries-old stone terracing" (1.8).

Similarly, the nation of Israel still exists in the world today. There are so many archaeological finds and historic documents which reference Israel, it would be impractical to try to present the breadth of our knowledge about Israel within this book. If you have an interest in Israel's extensive archaeology, I would suggest visiting: https://www.timesofisrael.com/topic/archaeology-in-israel/.

Because Elijah is an ancient figure, we have little in the way of archaeological evidence confirming his existence. However, there is a cave which is associated with the prophet Elijah.

"The Cave of Elijah is a large natural cavern in a sloping rocky outcrop at the foot of Mount Carmel, 131 feet above the sea, on the west side of the modern Israeli city of Haifa. In ancient times, what is now called the Cave of Elijah the Prophet was a place where believers practiced the cult of the pagan god Ba'al. The cave later became the site where Elijah was said to have rested before his bloody showdown with the prophets of Ba'al. From the Byzantine period on, the Cave of Elijah the Prophet was a stopping place and sanctuary for pilgrims and travelers who carved their inscriptions into its walls" (1.9).

Galilee and Nazareth are both regions still existing in today's world, so I won't delve into archaeology proving the existence of these places. We will cover specific aspects of the region of Galilee and archaeological finds which relate directly to Jesus in later chapters.

When it comes to Joseph, father of Jesus, there's an archaeological home site which has traditionally been respected and protected as Jesus's childhood home. While there is no indisputable evidence, such as having items with Joseph's, Mary's, or Jesus's names there, we also have no real reason to think ancient people picked the wrong home site to protect throughout history. After all, other ancient home sites have been let go as being of no consequence, and this is the only one singled out as Joseph's home.

As far as the historical home site goes, "The structure is exceptionally well-preserved because the builders of both Byzantine and Crusader churches (roughly contemporary with the churches of the Annunciation next door) made great efforts to encompass the remains of this building. It seems quite likely, (archaeologist) Dark argues, based on not only archaeological evidence but also on very ancient pilgrim descriptions, that the builders of the Byzantine church on the site — many centuries closer to the time of Jesus Christ than we are — believed themselves to be preserving and protecting the home of Joseph and Mary, the place where Jesus spent his childhood in Nazareth" (1.10).

This home site is one piece of evidence no one can know for certain whether it is actually Jesus' childhood home. Therefore, your decision for or against the authenticity of the home site is what matters most to you. Decide whether you think it's reasonable for the ancient people, who first preserved the home site, to know it was actually Mary and Joseph's home. Would they have preserved it if it was not?

In reference to Mary, mother of Jesus, "There is a tomb at the foot of the Mount of Olives in the Kidron Valley in Jerusalem which is traditionally said to be Mary's burial location" (1.4). "Since the early beginnings of Christianity, Mary's supposed tomb has been considered a sacred site. The tomb was excavated in 1972 by Bellarmino Bagatti, an archaeologist and Franciscan friar. He believed that the site is an ancient cemetery dating back to the 1st century A.D" (1.4).

"According to the 'Acts of St. John by Prochurus', written (160-70) by Lencius, the Evangelist went to Ephesus accompanied by Prochurus alone and at a very advanced age, i.e. after Mary's death. The two letters 'B. Inatii missa S. Joanni', written about 370, show that the Blessed Virgin passed the remainder of her days at Jerusalem" (1.5).

Thus, we have ancient archaeological sites and historical documents referencing the Virgin Mary, Jesus's mother, and the site preserved as Jesus's childhood home.

Our next mention of a person is King David. Very few people would debate the existence of King David as a real person. Aside from being mentioned throughout the Bible, we have archaeology and evidence supporting King David as a real person.

One piece of evidence is the Tel Dan tablet. "Few modern Biblical archaeology discoveries have caused as much excitement as the Tel Dan inscription—writing on a ninth-century B.C. stone slab (or stela) that furnished the first historical evidence of King David from the Bible. The Tel Dan inscription, or 'House of David' inscription, was discovered in 1993 at the site of Tel Dan in northern Israel in an excavation directed by Israeli archaeologist Avraham Biran" (1.11). Because of the dating of this tablet, its location, and the historical information we have about King David, we can be assured that he was a real person who lived in antiquity.

While we don't have direct evidence for Jacob, we do have evidence of several of his sons, which support the Biblical record concerning Jacob, his 12 sons, and the tribes of Israel. There's also evidence of the Israelites' time in Eqypt (1.12). Because Jacob had 12 sons, I won't list the evidence here, but would encourage you to read about the evidence at: https://christiananswers.net/q-abr/abr-a028.html.

"Abraham is considered to be the spiritual father of the world's three great monotheistic religions, Judaism, Christianity, and Islam" (1.13). "French archaeologists looking for Mari dug through centuries of sand to uncover Zimri-Lim's former palace. Deep within the ruins, they discovered tablets written in an ancient cuneiform script, one of the first forms of writing" (1.13). The tablets have been dated to the time Abraham's family left Ur.

"Some of the Mari tablets use words from the Amorite tribes that are also found in Abraham's story, such as his father's name, Terah, and his brothers' names, Nahor and Haran. From these artifacts and others, some scholars have concluded that Abraham's family may have been Amorites, a Semitic tribe that began to migrate out of Mesopotamia around 2100 B.C" (1.13). These ancient tablets give us solid evidence for the existence of Abraham's family clan. When combined with our knowledge in the Bible, we can be relatively certain Abraham was a real person.

WHAT DO YOU THINK?

➤ What kinds of things make you believe in or doubt there is a spiritual world?

_____
_____
_____
_____
_____
_____
_____

➤ Why do you think people believe Herod the Great is real, based on archaeological evidence, yet question the existence of Jesus as a real person within the same era?

_____
_____
_____
_____
_____
_____
_____

➢ If people believe there is a God who can do anything, why is Elizabeth's pregnancy more believable than Mary's, when the angel Gabriel told both women they would bear a son?

➢ If you were investigating the circumstances surrounding Mary's and Elizabeth's pregnancies who would you interview? Why would you choose those particular people?

➢ Why do you think fear came over all who lived around Zacharias and Elizabeth? How can fear strengthen and make a person's eyewitness testimony more reliable?

➤ Is there anything in this historical account of Zacharias, Elizabeth, and the birth of John the Baptist which increases your belief that these were real people who lived long ago? What portions of the story challenge your beliefs and why?

_____
_____
_____
_____
_____
_____
_____
_____

➤ If archaeological sites, such as Mary and Joseph's home and Mary's tomb, have been preserved from antiquity forward as being sacred historical sites, why do people now doubt what was unquestioned for thousands of years? What makes modern day people doubt ancient people's historical accounts and think today's people are wiser than all of the generations before them?

_____
_____
_____
_____
_____
_____
_____
_____

➤ In the Old Testament, God promised a descendant of David would be born and establish an everlasting Kingdom. What evidence do you see that Jesus established an everlasting kingdom?

_____
_____
_____
_____
_____
_____
_____
_____

CHAPTER 2

Now in those days, a decree went out from Caesar Augustus that all the world should be enrolled. This was the first enrollment made when Quirinius was governor of Syria. All went to enroll themselves, everyone to his own city. Joseph also went up from Galilee, out of the city of Nazareth, into Judea, to David's city, which is called Bethlehem, because he was of the house and family of David; to enroll himself with Mary, who was pledged to be married to him as wife, being pregnant.

While they were there, the day had come for her to give birth. She gave birth to her firstborn son. She wrapped him in bands of cloth, and laid him in a feeding trough, because there was no room for them in the inn. There were shepherds in the same country staying in the field, and keeping watch by night over their flock. Behold, an angel of the Lord stood by them, and the glory of the Lord shone around them, and they were terrified. The angel said to them, "Don't be afraid, for behold, I bring you good news of great joy which will be to all the people. For there is born to you today, in David's city, a Savior, who is Christ the Lord. This is the sign to you: you will find a baby wrapped in strips of cloth, lying in a feeding trough."

Suddenly, there was with the angel a multitude of the heavenly army praising God, and saying, "Glory to God in the highest, on earth peace, good will toward men."

When the angels went away from them into the sky, the shepherds said to one another, "Let's go to Bethlehem, now, and see this thing that has happened, which the Lord has made known to us." They came with haste, and found both Mary and Joseph, and the baby was lying in the feeding trough. When they saw it, they publicized widely the saying which was spoken to them about this child. All who heard it wondered at the things which were spoken to them by the shepherds. But Mary kept all these sayings, pondering them in her heart. The shepherds returned, glorifying and praising God for all the things that they had heard and seen, just as it was told them.

When eight days were fulfilled for the circumcision of the child, his name was called Jesus, which was given by the angel before he was conceived in the womb.

When the days of their purification according to the law of Moses were fulfilled, they brought him up to Jerusalem, to present him to the Lord (as it is written in the law of the Lord, "Every male who opens the womb shall be called holy to the Lord"), and to offer a sacrifice according to that which is said in the law of the Lord, "A pair of turtledoves, or two young pigeons."

Behold, there was a man in Jerusalem whose name was Simeon. This man was righteous and devout, looking for the consolation of Israel, and the Holy Spirit was on him. It had been revealed to him by the Holy Spirit that he should not see death before he had seen the Lord's Christ. He came in the Spirit into the temple. When the parents brought in the child, Jesus, that they might do concerning him according to the custom of the law, then he received him into his arms, and blessed God, and said, "Now you are releasing your servant, Master, according to your word, in peace; for my eyes have seen your salvation, which you have prepared before the face of all peoples; a light for revelation to the nations, and the glory of your people Israel."

Joseph and his mother were marveling at the things which were spoken concerning him, and Simeon blessed them, and said to Mary, his mother, "Behold, this child is set for the falling and the rising of many in Israel, and for a sign which is spoken against. Yes, a sword will pierce through your own soul, that the thoughts of many hearts may be revealed."

There was one Anna, a prophetess, the daughter of Phanuel, of the tribe of Asher (she was of a great age, having lived with a husband seven years from her virginity, and she had been a widow for about eighty-four years), who didn't depart from the temple, worshiping with fasting and petitions night and day. Coming up at that very hour, she gave thanks to the Lord, and spoke of him to all those who were looking for redemption in Jerusalem.

When they had accomplished all things that were according to the law of the Lord, they returned into Galilee, to their own city, Nazareth. The child was growing, and was becoming strong in spirit, being filled with wisdom, and the grace of God was upon him. His parents went every year to Jerusalem at the feast of the Passover.

When he was twelve years old, they went up to Jerusalem according to the custom of the feast, and when they had fulfilled the days, as they were returning, the boy Jesus stayed behind in Jerusalem. Joseph and his mother didn't know it, but supposing him to be in the company, they went a day's journey, and they looked for him among their relatives and acquaintances. When they didn't find him, they returned to Jerusalem, looking for him. After three days they found him in the temple, sitting in the middle of the teachers, both listening to them, and asking them questions. All who heard him were amazed at his understanding and his answers. When they saw him, they were astonished, and his mother said to him, "Son, why have you treated us this way? Behold, your father and I were anxiously looking for you."

He said to them, *"Why were you looking for me? Didn't you know that I must be in my Father's house?"*

They didn't understand the saying which he spoke to them. And he went down with them, and came to Nazareth. He was subject to them, and his mother kept all these sayings in her heart. And Jesus increased in wisdom and stature, and in favor with God and men.

ARCHAEOLOGICAL AND HISTORICAL EVIDENCE:

Caesar Augustus was the first emperor of the Roman Empire while Quintarius was the governor of Syria. Both Augustus and Quintarius are documented historical figures who died while Jesus was alive.

One piece of evidence we have regarding Caesar Augustus is an inscription found in Priene. "The Calendar Inscription of Priene speaks of the birthday of Caesar Augustus as the beginning of the gospel announcing his kingdom, with a Roman decree to start a new calendar system based on the year of Augustus Caesar's birth" (2.4). Augustus Caesar's birthdate was September 23, 63 B.C. You can read more information about Caesar Augustus at: https://www.romanemperors.com/augustus.htm (2.1).

"Archaeological discoveries in the 19th century reveal that Quirinius (or someone with the same name) was also a proconsul of Syria and Cilicia from 11 B.C. to the death of Herod. Quirinius' name has also been discovered on a coin from this period of time, and on the base of a statue erected in Pisidian Antioch" (2.5).

Syria, Bethlehem, and Jerusalem are mentioned in this chapter. Locations by the same names still exist in the world today. As with other places mentioned in the Bible which still exist today, we won't dig into the archaeological proof of their existence, except to make this note of one archaeological find that confirms the antiquity of Jerusalem:

"Archeologists uncovered an inscription on a pillar in an excavation of an ancient potter's village, near the western edge of the modern city of Jerusalem earlier this year. The inscription includes the word, "Yerushalayim," the name of Jerusalem written in Hebrew, and was dated to 100 B.C." (2.2).

Keep in mind all of the ancient cities listed above are great places where you may want to research the archaeological finds for Biblically related artifacts. In cities as old as Syria, Bethlehem, and Jerusalem, there's too much evidence to document without writing another book!

While we don't have direct evidence for Moses as an individual person, the Biblical Archaeology Review 42:3, May/June 2016, has Exodus Evidence: An Egyptologist Looks at Biblical History, an article which concludes, "Egyptian artifacts and sites show that the Biblical text does indeed recount accurate memories from the period to which the Exodus is generally assigned" (2.6).

"In the article, evidence is presented that generally supports a 13th-century B.C. Exodus during the Ramesside Period, when Egypt's 19th Dynasty ruled" (2.7). "Dated to c. 1219 B.C., the Merneptah Stele is the earliest extra-biblical record of a people group called Israel. Set up by Pharaoh Merneptah to commemorate his military victories, the stele proclaims, 'Ashkelon is carried off, and Gezer is captured. Yeno'am is made into nonexistence; Israel is wasted, its seed is not'" (2.7). This is very early evidence of the Egyptian Pharaoh's defeat of a people group called Israel.

Because the events took place so long ago, "Archaeological discoveries have verified that parts of the Biblical Exodus are historically accurate, but archaeology can't tell us everything" (2.7). For example, the archaeology and Egyptian records have not confirmed a man specifically named Moses, yet the Israelite's Torah is an ancient document that credits Moses with leading the Israelites in their exodus from Egypt.

Since the role and reality of Moses in ancient history hasn't been found carved in artifacts from the era, there's a lot of ongoing debate surrounding the historical facts about Moses and the exodus. However, the archaeological evidence we have does coincide with the Biblical narratives. The Institute for Biblical & Scientific Studies' article, Biblical Archaeology: Evidence of the Exodus from Egypt, at: https://www.bibleandscience.com/archaeology/exodus.htm has a great archaeological review of the evidence, if you want to explore the topic further.

We don't have any direct evidence for Simeon or Anna, who first recognized Jesus as the Messiah. Nor do we have evidence of Anna's father, Phanuel. However, we do know Anna and her father were from the tribe of Asher. We discussed the tribes of Jacob's sons in chapter 1, of which Asher is one of the sons and one of the twelve tribes (see 1.12). While we have concrete evidence for several of the twelve tribes, the individual tribe of Asher is not yet solidified in archeological findings.

A question for you to ponder would be whether Asher would be a made up tribe, even though the other tribes of Israel are verified in archaeology. Is it likely one of Jacob's 12 sons would be fictional?

We talked about Jesus' childhood home in the notes for Chapter 1. "The excavation site located beneath the Sisters of Nazareth Convent has been known since 1880, but it was never professionally excavated until the Nazareth Archaeological Project began its work in 2006.. Archaeological and geographical evidence from the Church of the Annunciation, the International Marion Center and Mary's Well come together to suggest that this location may be where Jesus transitioned from boy to man" (2.3).

While doubters point out it is impossible to know if the home is the location where Jesus grew up, the site is where the Sisters of Nazareth Convent was built *because* of the historical significance of the site. As we pondered in the previous chapter, a good question to consider would be why the site has been preserved throughout antiquity as Jesus's home, if Jesus wasn't a real person.

WHAT DO YOU THINK?

➤ Even though the gospels are four separate books, written by four different authors, who document Jesus's existence, why do you think people don't question Caesar Augustus's reign, yet they continue to question whether Jesus existed at all?

_____
_____
_____
_____
_____
_____
_____
_____

➤ Angels told the shepherds Jesus was a savior for all people, and they spread this news widely. Jesus became like a royal baby. Many people watched Him from birth onward to see what would become of him. Knowing this, how easy do you think it was for Luke to find witnesses to interview for his investigative report? How does this affect your feelings about the credibility of Luke's book?

_____
_____
_____
_____
_____
_____
_____
_____

➤ Jesus was born in Bethlehem, and Jerusalem is only 5.8 miles away from Bethlehem. In 8 days from Jesus' birth to the sacrificial offering for Jesus, how and why do you think the news from the Shepherds (about Jesus being the Savior) spread and reached the ears of Simeon in Jerusalem?

_____
_____
_____
_____
_____
_____
_____

➢ If you were Mary or Joseph, what might you think about what was being said about Jesus by the shepherds, Anna, and Simeon?

➢ Based on their actions following Mary's pregnancy, the sacrificial offering for Jesus on his 8th day, and their yearly trips to Jerusalem for Passover, how devout do you think Mary and Joseph were in their Jewish faith? What level of religious influence do you think Mary's and Joseph's faith had on Jesus while raising him?

➢ At the age of 13, Jewish boys become responsible for their own actions. In ancient times they were considered to be a legal adult at the age of 13. How do you think Jesus's status as legal adult affected Jesus's and his parents' thinking in the incident where Jesus stayed behind in the temple?

➢ What do you think is the origin of our human soul, spirit, and thoughts? Consider a single cell's simple structure. How can individual cells in our brains suddenly give us a personality, the ability to realize or know things, feelings, insights, etc. when they are still individual cells?

➢ How do you think the Holy Spirit relates to that which makes a person's soul and spirit within?

CHAPTER 3

Now in the fifteenth year of the reign of Tiberius Caesar, Pontius Pilate being governor of Judea, and Herod being tetrarch of Galilee, and his brother Philip tetrarch of the region of Ituraea and Trachonitis, and Lysanias tetrarch of Abilene, in the high priesthood of Annas and Caiaphas, the word of God came to John, the son of Zacharias, in the wilderness. He came into all the region around the Jordan, preaching the baptism of repentance for remission of sins. As it is written in the book of the words of Isaiah the prophet,

"The voice of one crying in the wilderness, 'Make ready the way of the Lord. Make his paths straight. Every mountain and hill will be brought low. Every valley will be filled. The crooked will become straight, and the rough ways smooth. All flesh will see God's salvation.'"

He said therefore to the multitudes who went out to be baptized by him, "You offspring of vipers, who warned you to flee from the wrath to come? Therefore produce fruits worthy of repentance, and don't begin to say among yourselves, 'We have Abraham for our father;'

for I tell you that God is able to raise up children to Abraham from these stones! Even now the ax also lies at the root of the trees. Every tree therefore that doesn't produce good fruit is cut down, and thrown into the fire."

The multitudes asked him, "What then must we do?"

He answered them, "He who has two coats, let him give to him who has none. He who has food, let him do likewise."

Tax collectors also came to be baptized, and they said to him, "Teacher, what must we do?"

He said to them, "Collect no more than that which is appointed to you."

Soldiers also asked him, saying, "What about us?

What must we do?"

He said to them, "Extort from no one by violence, neither accuse anyone wrongfully. Be content with your wages."

As the people were in expectation, and all men reasoned in their hearts concerning John, whether perhaps he was the Christ, John answered them all, "I indeed baptize you with water, but he comes who is mightier than I, the strap of whose sandals I am not worthy to loosen. He will baptize you in the Holy Spirit and fire, whose fan is in his hand, and he will thoroughly cleanse his threshing floor, and will gather the wheat into his barn; but he will burn up the chaff with unquenchable fire."

Then with many other exhortations he preached good news to the people, but Herod the tetrarch, being reproved by him for Herodias, his brother's wife, and for all the evil things which Herod had done, added this also to them all, that he shut up John in prison.

Now when all the people were baptized, Jesus also had been baptized, and was praying. The sky was opened, and the Holy Spirit descended in a bodily form like a dove on him; and a voice came out of the sky, saying *"You are my beloved Son. In you I am well pleased."*

Jesus himself, when he began to teach, was

about thirty years old, being the son (as was supposed) of Joseph, the son of Heli, the son of Matthat, the son of Levi, the son of Melchi, the son of Jannai, the son of Joseph, the son of Mattathias, the son of Amos, the son of Nahum, the son of Esli, the son of Naggai, the son of Maath, the son of Mattathias, the son of Semein, the son of Joseph, the son of Judah, the son of Joanan, the son of Rhesa, the son of Zerubbabel, the son of Shealtiel, the son of Neri, the son of Melchi, the son of Addi, the son of Cosam, the son of Elmodam, the son of Er, the son of Jose, the son of Eliezer, the son of Jorim, the son of Matthat, the son of Levi, the son of Simeon, the son of Judah, the son of Joseph, the son of Jonan, the son of Eliakim, the son of Melea, the son of Menan, the son of Mattatha, the son of Nathan, the son of David, the son of Jesse, the son of Obed, the son of Boaz, the son of Salmon, the son of Nahshon, the son of Amminadab, the son of Aram, the son of Hezron, the son of Perez, the son of Judah, the son of Jacob, the son of Isaac, the son of Abraham, the son of Terah, the son of Nahor, the son of Serug, the son of Reu, the son of Peleg, the son of Eber, the son of Shelah, the son of Cainan, the son of Arphaxad, the son of Shem, the son of Noah, the son of Lamech, the son of Methuselah, the son of Enoch, the son of Jared, the son of Mahalaleel, the son of Cainan, the son of Enos, the son of Seth, the son of Adam, the son of God.

ARCHAEOLOGICAL AND HISTORICAL EVIDENCE:

With this chapter's reference to Tiberius Caesar, we have another documented historical person who reigned 4-37 A.D., during Jesus's life. Tiberius and Pontius Pilate's names are set in stone on an ancient plaque, stating "Pontius Pilate, prefect of Judea, has dedicated to the people of Caesarea, a temple in the honor of Tiberius" (3.2). There are ancient coins from Tiberius as well. Herod, Philip, and Lysanias are referenced historical men, who help set the specific time frame for the events in this chapter of Luke's investigative reporting (3.1).

The Herodian Tetrarchy was formed following the death of Herod the Great in 4 B.C. His kingdom was divided between his sons Herod Achelous, Herod Antipas, and Philip, while Herod's sister Salome I ruled an area of Jamnia (3.5, 3.7).

When it comes to historical documentation about the Herodian dynasty, "Mykytiuk finds decisive documentation, primarily in the writings of the historian Flavius Josephus and in ancient minted coins, for the existence not only of Herod the Great but of his sons Herod Archelaus, Herod Antipas, Herod Philip and Philip the Tetrarch; his grandson Herod Agrippa I; his granddaughter Herodias; her daughter, Salome (named in Josephus, though not in the New Testament, where her infamous dance leads to the execution of John the Baptist); his great-grandson Herod Agrippa II, who, with Festus, listened to the apostle Paul's defense as described in Acts 25:13-26:32; his great-granddaughter Bernice or Berenice, the sister and perhaps the lover of Herod Agrippa II, who also attended Paul's defense; and his granddaughter Drusilla, who eventually married the Roman governor Felix" (3.8).

Lysanias, Tetrarch of Abilene, is one of the tetrarch's for which we do not have definite historical documentation or archaeological proof of his existence, but we do have possible evidence. "His identity is not clear enough in a relevant inscription to be certain he is the one referred to in Luke 3:1, but it is reasonable enough for some scholars to consider a New Testament identification probable. According to a dedicatory inscription carved in stone at Abila, capital city of the ancient tetrarchy of Abilene, a certain 'Lysanias the tetrarch, a freedman' ruled there" (Raphaël Savignac, 'Texte complet de l'inscription d'Abila relative à Lysanias,' Revue biblique, new series 9 [1912], pp. 533–540.) (3.9).

Ituraea and Trachonitis are two regions mentioned in this chapter. Ituraea is "located north of Mount Hermon and was the territory of the Ituraeans. After the death of Herod the Great, it became part of the Tetrarchy of Philip, son of Herod" (3.10).

"The name Trachonitis was described by Strabo (xvi, 2, 20) and comes from the two great stretches of lava, 'the tempests in stone,' which lie to the SE of Damascus-the Leja and the Safa. Philo used the name Trachonitis for the whole territory of Philip. Trachonitis was inhabited in New Testament times by turbulent tribes; conquered by Herod the Great and included in the Tetrarchy of Philip." (3.11)

"The territory of Abilene was a Roman district that extended over the slope of the anti-Lebanon, which was north of Mount Hermon. It was given the name after its capital city, Abila, which is situated in a gorge by the river Abanah (modern Barada), to the northwest of Damascus. Augustus assigned Abilene to Herod the Great, and after his death in four B.C. it was added to the province of Syria. By the time of the Emperor Tiberias (A.D. 14-37) it was in the Tetrarchy of Lysanias" (3.12).

Two high priests mentioned in this chapter of Luke are Annas and Caiaphas. "'Caiaphas' house has been located. It's up on the hill not far from our site,' Gibson points out in additional support of the thesis. 'We know from pilgrim reports that Caiaphas's house was in this area. The Armenian site is just up the hill from our site, the Roman Catholic site Peter Gallicanu is just below,' Prof. James Tabor of the University of North Carolina at Charlotte told Haaretz. 'Caiaphas was the son-in-law of Annas, who had six sons who were high priests. He ran the show for about 60 years putting his sons in one after the other, and his son-in-law, Caiaphas along the way. So perhaps these are the homes of that extended priestly dynasty,' Tabor said. The high priests at that time were notorious, with a reputation for being corrupt, brutal and greedy. We learn this from the Gospel accounts and from Talmudic texts" (3.13).

Archaeologists have found a small box bearing an inscription referencing John the Baptist. Carbon dating and DNA analysis of the bones found with the Box confirm the bones are those of a middle eastern man from the first century A.D. While the DNA and dating don't conclusively prove the bones are John the Baptist, logic and reasoning would lead most people to conclude the inscription combined with the DNA profile and dating evidence would point to John being a real person. The person, who was found in the box, was most likely John the Baptist, or alternatively someone related to him (3.4).

Many people trace their family trees. In his book, Luke presents Jesus's family tree. Some of the ancestors of Jesus, like King David, are archaeologically proven to be real individuals. An ossuary (a limestone casket) bears the inscription, "James, son of Joseph, brother of Jesus," and has been authenticated to be from the era of Jesus by world-class experts (3.6). This physical ossuary, with Jesus's name engraved on it, is a piece of solid evidence that Jesus was a real person who was worth mentioning in relation to James and Joseph.

The last physical location mentioned in this chapter of Luke is the Jordan river, which still exists today. Therefore, as with other places which have existed from Jesus's day until this day, we don't really need to prove the Jordan River is a real place.

At the Jordan River, a historical site is preserved as the site of Jesus' baptism, which tourists visit with great frequency. "*Bethany Beyond the Jordan* is considered by the majority of the Christian Churches to be the location where John the Baptist baptized Jesus. The archaeological areas have been preserved in their original materials, but have in many places been restored adding similar materials from the area. In some cases archaeological fragments have been reassembled. However, the restorations do not affect the significance or credibility attributed to the site by Christian believers" (3.14).

WHAT DO YOU THINK?

➤ With the care Luke took to document precise historical details, having been called a historian of the first rank (3.3), and with archaeological evidence supporting the facts in Luke's historic account, what are your thoughts regarding the factual basis of Luke's report, so far?

_____
_____
_____
_____
_____
_____
_____
_____

➤ Luke investigates and reports about events documented through interviews and research. In any other context, people would believe Luke's report refers to real people and real events. Why do some people disregard Luke's report of facts and evidence simply because his book is one of 66 books chosen to be bound together to create the Bible?

_____
_____
_____
_____
_____
_____
_____
_____

➤ With the evidence we have for the existence of Jesus's ancestors and his brother, in addition to Old Testament and Jewish historical records, in what ways does Jesus's genealogy seem reasonable or real as presented in this chapter? (3.6) What, if anything, might make someone think it's fictional?

➤ The Bible is actually 66 separate books written by 40 different authors over the span of 1500 years. The books are bound together to provide a historical account of God's relationship with people from the beginning of time. Why do you think the inclusion of these books in the Bible makes people think they're completely fictional, rather than understanding each is a separate book written by an individual author, just like books written by Homer, Aristotle, Plato, and other ancient authors?

➤ When it comes to historic figures and people groups you know in the Old Testament, which people do you believe were real people? For example, Noah, Jonah, King David, King Solomon, Moses, Abraham, Esther, the Canaanites, the Israelites, etc. What makes you believe they are real people?

➤ Which major events in the Bible, of which you've heard, do you believe are actual events in history? (Exodus, Flood, Wars, etc.) Reflect on what you believe. Why do you believe the way you do?

CHAPTER 4

Jesus, full of the Holy Spirit, returned from the Jordan, and was led by the Spirit into the wilderness for forty days, being tempted by the devil. He ate nothing in those days. Afterward, when they were completed, he was hungry. The devil said to him, "If you are the Son of God, command this stone to become bread."

Jesus answered him, saying, *"It is written, 'Man shall not live by bread alone, but by every word of God.'"*

The devil, leading him up on a high mountain, showed him all the kingdoms of the world in a moment of time. The devil said to him, "I will give you all this authority, and their glory, for it has been delivered to me; and I give it to whomever I want. If you therefore will worship before me, it will all be yours."

Jesus answered him, *"Get behind me Satan! For it is written, 'You shall worship the Lord your God, and you shall serve him only.'"*

He led him to Jerusalem, and set him on the pinnacle of the temple, and said to him, "If you are the Son of God, cast yourself down from here, for it is written, 'He will put his angels in charge of you, to guard you;' and, 'On their hands they will bear you up, lest perhaps you dash your foot against a stone.'"

Jesus answering, said to him, *"It has been said, 'You shall not tempt the Lord your God.'"*

When the devil had completed every temptation, he departed from him until another time.

Jesus returned in the power of the Spirit into Galilee, and news about him spread through all the surrounding area. He taught in their synagogues, being glorified by all.

He came to Nazareth, where he had been brought up. He entered, as was his custom, into the synagogue on the Sabbath day, and stood up to read. The book of the prophet Isaiah was handed to him. He opened the book, and found the place where it was written,

"The Spirit of the Lord is on me, because he has anointed me to preach good news to the poor. He has sent me to heal the broken hearted, to proclaim release to the captives, recovering of sight to the blind, to deliver those who are crushed, and to proclaim the acceptable year of the Lord."

He closed the book, gave it back to the attendant, and sat down. The eyes of all in the synagogue were fastened on him. He began to tell them, *"Today, this Scripture has been fulfilled in your hearing."*

All testified about him, and wondered at the gracious words which proceeded out of his mouth, and they said, "Isn't this Joseph's son?"

He said to them, *"Doubtless you will tell me this parable, 'Physician, heal yourself! Whatever we have heard done at Capernaum, do also here in your hometown.'"* He said, *"Most certainly I tell you, no prophet is acceptable in his hometown. But truly I tell you, there were many widows in Israel in the days of Elijah, when the sky was shut up three years and six months, when a great famine came over all the land. Elijah was sent to none of them, except to Zarephath, in the land of*

Sidon, to a woman who was a widow. There were many lepers in Israel in the time of Elisha the prophet, yet not one of them was cleansed, except Naaman, the Syrian."

They were all filled with wrath in the synagogue, as they heard these things. They rose up, threw him out of the city, and led him to the brow of the hill that their city was built on, that they might throw him off the cliff. But he, passing through the middle of them, went his way.

He came down to Capernaum, a city of Galilee. He was teaching them on the Sabbath day, and they were astonished at his teaching, for his word was with authority. In the synagogue there was a man who had a spirit of an unclean demon, and he cried out with a loud voice, saying, "Ah! what have we to do with you, Jesus of Nazareth? Have you come to destroy us? I know who you are: the Holy One of God!"

Jesus rebuked him, saying, *"Be silent, and come out of him!"* When the demon had thrown him down in the middle of them, he came out of him, having done him no harm.

Amazement came on all, and they spoke together, one with another, saying, "What is this word? For with authority and power he commands the unclean spirits, and they come out!" News about him went out into every place of the surrounding region.

He rose up from the synagogue, and entered into Simon's house. Simon's mother-in-law was afflicted with a great fever, and they begged him for her. He stood over her, and rebuked the fever; and it left her. Immediately she rose up and served them. When the sun was setting, all those who had any sick with various diseases brought them to him; and he laid his hands on every one of them, and healed them. Demons also came out of many, crying out, and saying, "You are the Christ, the Son of God!" Rebuking them, he didn't allow them to speak, because they knew that he was the Christ.

When it was day, he departed and went into

an uninhabited place, and the multitudes looked for him, and came to him, and held on to him, so that he wouldn't go away from them. But he said to them, *"I must preach the good news of God's Kingdom to the other cities also. For this reason I have been sent."* He was preaching in the synagogues of Galilee.

ARCHAEOLOGICAL AND HISTORICAL EVIDENCE:

Archaeological digs in Capernaum confirm the city existed at the time Jesus was alive. The existence of Capernaum is also confirmed in writings by Josephus Flavius, who was a first century historian (4.1).

An archaeological excavation found a Christian home in Capernaum. The home has second Century writings on the walls referencing Jesus (4.1). The home is believed to be the Apostle Peter's home, as described by the Gospels and local tradition. The home was also close to the synagogue in Capernaum.

In addition there are two synagogues, one of which is one of the oldest in the world. It is mentioned in three of the four gospels, including this chapter. A 2000 year old fishing boat was preserved in the mud and found at Capernaum (4.1). It now resides in a museum in Galilee.

"The city-state of Sidon, twenty kilometers south of the Lebanese capital, Beirut, was one of the most important cities of the ancient Canaanite & Phoenician peoples. However, like other places in modern Lebanon, most of what we knew of its history until now came from contemporary Egyptian, Assyrian, Babylonian and Greek records" (4.2). In the current day, there are ongoing archaeological digs, which continue to advance our knowledge of the region through archaeology.

"The terms Sidon and Sidonians, found in the Old Testament thirty eight times were not only used in a narrow sense, of the city itself and its inhabitants but in a much wider sense, including at times Tyre and its inhabitants, and at others, the whole of Phoenicia" (4.2). Today, from both historical documents and archaeology, we know the regions of Sidon and Tyre were real places.

"Zarephath, whose Phoenician name was Sarepta, was a seaport lying on the Mediterranean coast between Sidon and Tyre. It thrived from about 1600 to 100 B.C. and occupied an area of 15 to 20 acres. Today Zarephath lies beneath the modern fishing village of Sarafand.

"Zarephath, the city where the prophet Elijah lived while hiding from King Ahab in the 9th century B.C. is again coming to life. It was during Elijah's stay with a widow woman there, that he miraculously multiplied her provisions and brought her son back to life (1 Kings 17). During the summer of 1972, Dr. Pritchard completed his fourth season of excavating at Zarephath under a six-year Lebanese permit (See BIBLE AND SPADE, Vol. 1, No. 1, pg. 21)" (4.3).

When it comes to the ancient prophet, Elisha, mentioned in this chapter, there is archaeological evidence of him as a living person. Aside from the Cave of Elisha, "Archaeologists in Israel have found a shard of pottery with the name of the Old Testament prophet Elisha on it, leading them to believe they have discovered his home. The pottery shard has been dated to the 9th century BC, which would have been the time he lived, and was found in a house uncovered in Tel Rehov in the Jordan Valley, just seven miles from where Elisha was born" (4.4).

Naaman, the Syrian, who was healed of Leprosy by Elisha, is a Biblical figure for which there is no known evidence, other than what is written in the Bible. Naaman was noteworthy for having been healed, but not for accomplishing any task which we would expect to see recorded in historical documents outside of the Bible or found in the archaeology. For most of the people Jesus healed, there are no archaeological records of them. We don't even know most of their names.

We do know that Naaman was a Syrian, and we talked about Syria in chapter two. Syria, again, is a real country which still exists today.

Simon, as mentioned in this chapter, is Simon Peter, the Apostle. At the beginning of this section, we discussed archaeological evidence for the city of Capernaum, and part of that evidence included a home that is considered (Simon) Peter's home. In the historical record, outside the Bible, "The earliest testimony to the apostle Peter's presence in Rome is a letter from a Christian deacon named Gaius. Writing probably toward the end of the second century B.C.—so, around 170 or 180 B.C.—Gaius tells about the wondrous things in Rome, including something called a tropaion (a memorial of sorts) where Peter established a church—in fact, the Church, the Roman Catholic church at the site where St. Peter's Basilica is today" (4.5). However, there is significant debate about whether Simon Peter was ever actually in Rome, as discussed in the 4.5 referenced article. Thus, it is virtually certain Simon Peter was a real person, but his actual location at the time of his death is debatable.

WHAT DO YOU THINK?

➤ Why do you think people wrote Jesus's name on walls in Capernaum during the first century after He lived? What level of importance would you give this evidence for the existence of Jesus and why?

➤ Jesus taught in the region surrounding Galilee, and news about him spread throughout the region. Jesus's notoriety enabled Luke to investigate and report about the events which occurred in Jesus's life. How accurate does Luke's reporting seem to you, and why do you think as you do?

➢ In this chapter, Jesus plainly states he has the Holy Spirit on him and the Lord has anointed Jesus to preach the good news. Jesus spoke; people marveled. What do you think it was which made Jesus and His teachings captivating to His audiences?

_____
_____
_____
_____
_____
_____
_____
_____

➢ Everyone loved and marveled at Jesus's wise teachings until he spoke the truth about their sinful thoughts. Then the people wanted to stone Jesus. What fears and emotions would make the people's love and amazement turn to anger and hatred in a short span of time?

_____
_____
_____
_____
_____
_____
_____
_____
_____
_____

➢ What do you think caused gossip about Jesus to spread to every place in the surrounding regions? Is the human propensity to gossip and spread news any different today than it was in Jesus's time? How is it the same and how is it different in today's world?

_____
_____
_____
_____
_____
_____
_____
_____
_____
_____

➤ Jesus's main goal was to preach God's good news. What is the good news, as you understand it?

➤ Jesus was a man, born of Mary, tempted by hunger, power, and challenging God. Jesus fought Satan's temptations by quoting Bible verses, which gave him strength to stand against Satan. What can we learn from Jesus about standing firm against temptations by memorizing Bible verses?

➤ What evil forces, if any, do you believe exist in the physical and spiritual world?

➤ If the Holy Spirit exists, what influence do you believe He has on the character of and in the lives of people who have an indwelling of the Holy Spirit?

CHAPTER 5

Now while the multitude pressed on him and heard the word of God, he was standing by the lake of Gennesaret. He saw two boats standing by the lake, but the fishermen had gone out of them, and were washing their nets. He entered into one of the boats, which was Simon's, and asked him to put out a little from the land. He sat down and taught the multitudes from the boat. When he had finished speaking, he said to Simon, *"Put out into the deep, and let down your nets for a catch."*

Simon answered him, "Master, we worked all night, and took nothing; but at your word I will let down the net." When they had done this, they caught a great multitude of fish, and their net was breaking. They beckoned to their partners in the other boat, that they should come and help them. They came, and filled both boats, so that they began to sink. But Simon Peter, when he saw it, fell down at Jesus' knees, saying, "Depart from me, for I am a sinful man, Lord." For he was amazed, and all who were with him, at the catch of fish which they had caught; and so also were James and John, sons of Zebedee, who were partners with Simon.

Jesus said to Simon, *"Don't be afraid. From now on you will be fishers of men."*

When they had brought their boats to land, they left everything, and followed him. While he was in one of the cities, behold, there was a man full of leprosy. When he saw Jesus, he fell on his face, and begged him, saying, "Lord, if you want to, you can make me clean."

He stretched out his hand, and touched him, saying, *"I want to. Be made clean."*

Immediately the leprosy left him. He commanded him to tell no one, *"But go your way, and show yourself to the priest, and offer for your cleansing according to what Moses commanded, for a testimony to them."* But the report concerning him spread much more, and great multitudes came together to hear, and to be healed by him of their infirmities. But he withdrew himself into the desert, and prayed.

On one of those days, he was teaching; and there were Pharisees and teachers of the law sitting by, who had come out of every village of Galilee, Judea, and Jerusalem. The power of the Lord was with him to heal them. Behold, men brought a paralyzed man on a cot and they sought to bring him in to lay before Jesus. Not finding a way to bring him in because of the multitude, they went up to the housetop, and let him down through the tiles with his cot into the middle before Jesus. Seeing their faith, he said to him, *"Man, your sins are forgiven you."*

The scribes and the Pharisees began to reason, saying, "Who is this that speaks blasphemies? Who can forgive sins, but God alone?"

But Jesus, perceiving their thoughts, answered them, *"Why are you reasoning so in your hearts? Which is easier to say, 'Your sins are forgiven you;' or to say, 'Arise and walk?' But that you may know that the Son of Man has authority on earth to forgive sins"* (he said to the paralyzed man), *"I tell you, arise, take up your cot, and go to your house."*

Immediately he rose up before them, and took up that which he was laying on, and departed to his house, glorifying God. Amazement took hold on all, and they glorified God. They were filled with fear, saying, "We have seen strange things today."

After these things he went out, and saw a tax collector named Levi sitting at the tax office, and said to him, *"Follow me!"*

He left everything, and rose up and followed him. Levi made a great feast for him in his house. There was a great crowd of tax collectors and others who were reclining with them. Their scribes and the Pharisees murmured against his disciples, saying, "Why do you eat and drink with the tax collectors and sinners?" Jesus answered them, *"Those who are healthy have no need for a physician, but those who are sick do. I have not come to call the righteous, but sinners to repentance."*

They said to him, "Why do John's disciples often fast and pray, likewise also the disciples of the Pharisees, but yours eat and drink?"

He said to them, *"Can you make the friends of the bridegroom fast while the bridegroom is with them? But the days will come when the bridegroom will be taken away from them. Then they will fast in those days."*

He also told a parable to them. *"No one puts a piece from a new garment on an old garment, or else he will tear the new, and also the piece from the new will not match the old. No one puts new wine into old wine skins, or else the new wine will burst the skins, and it will be spilled, and the skins will be destroyed. But new wine must be put into fresh wine skins, and both are preserved. No man having drunk old wine immediately desires new, for he says, 'The old is better.'"*

ARCHAEOLOGICAL AND HISTORICAL EVIDENCE:

The Pharisees were the influential religious leaders in Jesus's day, pursuing rigid righteousness based on following the letter of the law. There is a lot of documentation about the Pharisees as a religious sect within the Jewish religion.

Ancient historian, Josephus (37–circa 100 A.D.), "designates the Pharisees a 'sect' and a 'philosophy' distinguished by their belief in fate and the resurrection of the dead, their precision in studying the Torah, and their adherence to an extra-biblical 'tradition of the fathers.' On occasion he highlights their political activity, such as their influence during the reign of Salome Alexandra or their sway among the masses" (5.1).

"In the Mishnah (circa 200 A.D.) and Tosefta (circa 300 A.D.), the rabbis attribute many legal decisions to the Pharisees or to proto-rabbis widely recognized as Pharisees (for example, Hillel, Shammai, and Gamaliel), especially regarding tithing and purity" (5.1). Also see the 5.2 resource.

The Pharisees where influential from before Jesus lived, and lasting until around the 2nd Century A.D., after the Jewish temple was destroyed. After that time, Christianity became a significant religion.

In this chapter we are also introduced to the first few disciples. There are varying amounts of documentation and evidence for Jesus's disciples. I believe it will be best to cover most of their evidence later in this book, when the evidence we have more closely relates to the story at that point.

When it comes to James and John, the sons of Zebedee, and Matthew, we will talk about them at the very end of the book when we discuss historical evidence regarding the disciples' martyrdoms. Feel free to flip to the evidence notes at the end of the last chapter of this book to see what we know about the deaths of Matthew, James and John, if you want to know now.

WHAT DO YOU THINK?

➤ Within a short span of time, a multitude of people began following Jesus. What do you think the people were seeking or hoping for when they sought after Jesus?

___

➤ What impact do you think the constant presence of multitudes of people had on the spread of Jesus's message?

___

➢ Which of the three miracles performed in this chapter (the great fish catch, healing of leprosy, and the lame man being able to walk) do you feel is most believable? Why?

➢ The Pharisees and scribes began questioning, judging, and looking down on Jesus, yet Jesus's wisdom and insight amazed everyone. Why do you think people today continue questioning and judging Jesus in spite of His timeless wisdom? How well do you think people know Jesus today?

➢ As presented in the parable of the wine and the wineskins, why are people resistant to new ways of thinking? Why do they prefer to cling to old ways as being better? How can we determine which is actually better?

➢ How is the Pharisees' and scribes' judgement of Jesus likely to have affected people's opinions about Jesus? In what ways is your opinion of other people likely to be influenced by the opinions of those with whom you associate?

_____
_____
_____
_____
_____
_____
_____
_____

➢ People sometimes think Christianity began as a small movement among 12 men who followed Jesus. However, multitudes learned from and followed Jesus in His day; the 12 disciples were just Jesus's Inner Circle. In what ways is it more supernatural than natural for the number of people following Jesus to continue to grow throughout the centuries, including gaining followers in the world today?

_____
_____
_____
_____
_____
_____
_____
_____
_____

➢ If Jesus is all-knowing and has all of the wisdom of the world, in what areas of your life would you benefit from receiving wisdom and insight from Jesus?

_____
_____
_____
_____
_____
_____
_____
_____
_____

CHAPTER 6

Now on the second Sabbath after the first, he was going through the grain fields. His disciples plucked the heads of grain and ate, rubbing them in their hands. But some of the Pharisees said to them, "Why do you do that which is not lawful to do on the Sabbath day?"

Jesus, answering them, said, *"Haven't you read what David did when he was hungry, he, and those who were with him; how he entered into God's house, and took and ate the show bread, and gave also to those who were with him, which is not lawful to eat except for the priests alone?"* He said to them, *"The Son of Man is lord of the Sabbath."*

It also happened on another Sabbath that he entered into the synagogue and taught. There was a man there, and his right hand was withered. The scribes and the Pharisees watched him, to see whether he would heal on the Sabbath, that they might find an accusation against him. But he knew their thoughts; and he said to the man who had the withered hand, *"Rise up, and stand in the middle."* He arose and stood. Then Jesus said to them, *"I will ask you something: Is it lawful on the Sabbath to do good, or to do harm? To save a life, or to kill?"* He looked around at them all, and said to the man, *"Stretch out your hand."* He did, and his hand was restored as sound as the other. But they were filled with rage, and talked with one another about what they might do to Jesus.

In these days, he went out to the mountain to pray, and he continued all night in prayer to God. When it was day, he called his disciples, and from them he chose twelve, whom he also named apostles: Simon, whom he also named Peter; Andrew, his brother; James; John; Philip; Bartholomew; Matthew; Thomas; James, the son of Alphaeus; Simon, who was called the Zealot; Judas the son of James; and Judas Iscariot, who also became a traitor. He came down with them, and stood on a level place, with a crowd of his disciples, and a great number of the people from all Judea and Jerusalem, and the sea coast of Tyre and Sidon, who came to hear him and to be healed of their diseases; as well as those who were troubled by unclean spirits, and they were being healed. All the multitude sought to touch him, for power came out of him and healed them all.

He lifted up his eyes to his disciples, and said, *"Blessed are you who are poor, God's Kingdom is yours.*

Blessed are you who hunger now, for you will be filled.

Blessed are you who weep now, for you will laugh.

Blessed are you when men hate you, and when they exclude and mock you, and throw out your name as evil, for the Son of Man's sake.

Rejoice in that day, and leap for joy, for behold, your reward is great in heaven, for their fathers did the same thing to the prophets.

But woe to you who are rich! For you have received your consolation.

Woe to you, you who are full now, for you will be hungry.

Woe to you who laugh now, for you will mourn and weep.

Woe, when men speak well of you, for their fathers did the same thing to the false prophets.

"But I tell you who hear: love your enemies, do good to those who hate you, bless those who curse you, and pray for those who mistreat you. To him who strikes you on the cheek, offer also the other; and from him who takes away your cloak, don't withhold your coat also. Give to everyone who asks you, and don't ask him who takes away your goods to give them back again.

"As you would like people to do to you, do exactly so to them. If you love those who love you, what credit is that to you? For even sinners love those who love them. If you do good to those who do good to you, what credit is that to you? For even sinners do the same. If you lend to those from whom you hope to receive, what credit is that to you? Even sinners lend to sinners, to receive back as much. But love your enemies, and do good, and lend, expecting nothing back; and your reward will be great, and you will be children of the Most High; for he is kind toward the unthankful and evil.

"Therefore be merciful, even as your Father is also merciful.

Don't judge, and you won't be judged.

Don't condemn, and you won't be condemned.

Set free, and you will be set free.

"Give, and it will be given to you: good measure, pressed down, shaken together, and running over, will be given to you. For with the same measure you measure it will be measured back to you."

He spoke a parable to them. *"Can the blind guide the blind? Won't they both fall into a pit? A disciple is not above his teacher, but everyone when he is fully trained will be like his teacher. Why do you see the speck of chaff that is in your brother's eye, but don't consider the beam that is in your own eye? Or how can you tell your brother, 'Brother, let me remove the speck of chaff that is in your eye,' when you yourself don't see the beam that is in your own eye? You hypocrite! First remove the beam from your own eye, and then you can see clearly to remove the speck of chaff that is in your brother's eye. For there is no good tree that produces rotten fruit; nor again a rotten tree that produces good fruit. For each tree is known by its own fruit. For people don't gather figs from thorns, nor do they gather grapes from a bramble bush. The good man out of the good treasure of his heart brings out that which is good, and the evil man out of the evil treasure of his heart brings out that which is evil, for out of the abundance of the heart, his mouth speaks.*

"Why do you call me, 'Lord, Lord,' and don't do the things which I say? Everyone who comes to me, and hears my words, and does them, I will show you who he is like. He is like a man building a house, who dug and went deep, and laid a foundation on the rock. When a flood arose, the stream broke against that house, and could not shake it, because it was founded on the rock. But he who hears, and doesn't do, is like a man who built a house on the earth without a foundation, against which the stream broke, and immediately it fell, and the ruin of that house was great."

ARCHAEOLOGICAL AND HISTORICAL EVIDENCE:

We have been introduced to all 12 disciples. It's interesting that we have historical evidence for the location of almost all of the disciples' artifacts (bones) after their deaths. Where are the disciples today?

An article titled "Where Are the 12 Apostles Now?" gives information about the deaths and dispositions for the artifacts of each of Jesus's Apostles. I'll provide a summary listing of the current location of the relics of each Apostle below, but I highly recommend reading the full article for an understanding of what we know versus what is speculated. If you want to read the full article, it is located at: http://m.ncregister.com/blog/tcraughwell/where-are-the-12-apostles-now.

Simon Peter (Peter) – "About the year 64, St. Peter was crucified head downward in the Circus, or Arena, of Nero on the Vatican Hill. Christians recovered his body and buried it in a nearby cemetery. About the year 326 the Emperor Constantine leveled what remained of the arena, and the hill, and erected a large basilica with the high altar positioned above St. Peter's grave. But after centuries of restorations and reconstructions, the location of the grave became lost. Tradition continued to insist that Peter's bones lay beneath the high altar of his basilica, but no one had seen it in centuries.

"In 1939, workmen were digging a grave for Pope Pius XI in the grottoes under St. Peter's when one of them felt his shovel cut into a void rather than dirt. Shining a flashlight through the hole, the work crew saw the interior of a second-century mausoleum. Directly beneath the high altar of St. Peter's, archaeologists found a simple tomb containing the bones of a robust, elderly man. Scratched into the tomb wall were countless prayers and petitions to St. Peter, as well as a Greek inscription that read, *'Peter is within.'* After years of study, Blessed Pope Paul VI declared in 1968 that the bones in that tomb were those of St. Peter" (6.1).

Paul – "remains are enshrined in a sarcophagus beneath the high altar of Rome's Basilica of St. Paul Outside-the-Walls."

John - is missing. In the 1920s, archaeologists found John's "tomb was empty, and no one knows what became of John's body."

Andrew - was carried to Amalfi, in 1204 by Italian Crusaders who looted St. Andrew's shrine. Amalfi is where Andrew's relics remain to this day.

James, son of Zebedee - is "enshrined in the magnificent Cathedral of St. James in Santiago de Compostela."

James, son of Alphaeus - was moved to the Church of the Twelve Apostles in Rome, where today he lies in the same shrine with the relics of his fellow apostle, St. Philip.

Philip - is with James, still venerated in the crypt of the Twelve Apostles in Rome (See also 6.3).

Thomas - is divided. "A portion of St. Thomas' bones are venerated in the Basilica of St. Thomas in Chennai, India." The rest of St. Thomas's relics are in Ortona, Italy, "where they lie today enshrined in a golden casket within a white marble altar in the Basilica of St. Thomas the Apostle."

Bartholomew - was taken "in 838 to Benevento in southern Italy. In 983 the Holy Roman Emperor, Otto III, erected in Rome a church on Tiberina Island in the Tiber River; he dedicated the church to St. Bartholomew and had a portion of the apostle's relics enshrined there. So both Rome and Benevento are the major shrines of St. Batholomew."

Matthew - Is in "the city of Salerno in Italy. The relics are venerated in the crypt of Salerno's Cathedral of St. Matthew."

Simon and Jude - are at Rome's Basilica of St. Peter, where an altar holds the relics of St. Jude and St. Simon.

Please refer to the "Where Are the 12 Apostles Now?" (6.1) article for more extensive details about each of the Apostles' deaths and burials. We will talk about the deaths of the disciples at the very end of the book, as well as at other points within the book.

In Jerusalem, Israel, "Archaeologists say they have likely found the Church of the Apostles in ancient Bethsaida, which is believed to have been built over the home of Jesus' disciples, Peter and Andrew. 'There is a document from a visitor from the end of the 7th century AD, a Christian pilgrim, [which] says that after he left Capernaum, he arrived to Bethsaida, and there is a church for the apostles, Peter and Andrew,' Aviam explained. 'Also we used drones and also ground machinery with electromagnetic sensors. With this, we discovered that the entire area around where we excavated these houses is full of (more) houses.'" (6.2).

For Judas, son of James, we have a piece of historical documentation. Josephus mentions Judas and his sons in ancient Jewish records. Josephus writes, "Fadus became procurator, succeeding Tiberius Alexander, and he crucified Simon and James, the sons of Judas, the Galilean who had led the people to revolt during the time Quirinius was taking a census in the land of Judea" (6.4).

Josephus's paragraph provides a tiny snapshot of one event in the life of Judas. Josephus was a Jewish historian, born around the time of Jesus's death, who lived throughout the rest of the first century. Josephus' writings provide independent historical documentation about a great number of things during the first century in the region around Jerusalem, including the disciples and events related to Christians.

We will learn more about Simon, Judas son of James, and Judas Iscariot in chapter 22 of this book.

Lastly, in this chapter, we have the mention of Tyre, an ancient city in the region. Tyre has been around since 2750 BC, and still exists today. "Whereas Roman and Medieval remains are still visible throughout the modern city, archaeological excavations have reached levels dating back to the 3rd millennium B.C." (6.5). So, Tyre has been around since Old Testament times!

WHAT DO YOU THINK?

➢ The Pharisees were legalistic about doing no work on the Sabbath; Jesus was more relaxed about doing good on the Sabbath. What do you think makes people legalistic about religious matters? What is the difference between doing good on the Sabbath versus working on the Sabbath?

➢ The Pharisees sought accusations against Jesus and thought they were more righteous than Jesus. How is the Pharisee's behavior similar to self-righteous people's behavior today? (Consider atheists who think themselves better than Christians, Christians who think they're better than unreligious people, and people in other religions who think themselves better than others.) Why is self-righteousness a prevalent problem among virtually every people group?

➢ In this chapter, Jesus is described as being followed by his Twelve Apostles, a crowd of disciples, and a great number of people from all Judea, Jerusalem, the coast of Tyre, and Sidon. What kind of reaction would you expect from all of Jesus' followers, who believe He is the Messiah, when Jesus is crucified, actually dies, and is placed in a tomb? What would you expect them to do and think?

_____
_____
_____
_____
_____
_____
_____
_____
_____

➢ Chapter 6 says, "All the multitude sought to touch him, for power came out of him and healed them all." Clearly a great number of people believed Jesus had the power to heal. Between those who believed Jesus was God's son and those who sought to destroy him, what would be the primary reason(s) for the differences in their beliefs about Jesus?

_____
_____
_____
_____
_____
_____
_____
_____
_____

➢ Jesus says, "As you would like people to do to you, do exactly to them," "with the same measure you measure, it will be measured back to you," and "Love your enemies." How is Jesus's wisdom about living righteously unlike teachings from typical leaders and teachers throughout history?

_____
_____
_____
_____
_____
_____
_____
_____
_____

- Do Jesus's teachings and His wisdom seem supernatural or like that of an ordinary human? Why do feel that way?

- Jesus's teachings and commands are simple and easily understood. Why do you think it is so difficult for people to whole-heartedly do everything Jesus teaches us?

- When you consider what our Creator God is likely to expect from us, is there anything unexpected in Jesus' teachings? What do you think our difficulty in following Jesus' commands reveals about our ability to be completely righteous in God's eyes?

CHAPTER 7

After he had finished speaking in the hearing of the people, he entered into Capernaum. A certain centurion's servant, who was dear to him, was sick and at the point of death. When he heard about Jesus, he sent to him elders of the Jews, asking him to come and save his servant. When they came to Jesus, they begged him earnestly, saying, "He is worthy for you to do this for him, for he loves our nation, and he built our synagogue for us." Jesus went with them.

When he was now not far from the house, the centurion sent friends to him, saying to him, "Lord, don't trouble yourself, for I am not worthy for you to come under my roof. Therefore I didn't even think myself worthy to come to you; but say the word, and my servant will be healed. For I also am a man placed under authority, having under myself soldiers. I tell this one, 'Go!' and he goes; and to another, 'Come!' and he comes; and to my servant, 'Do this,' and he does it."

When Jesus heard these things, he marveled at him, and turned and said to the multitude who followed him, *"I tell you, I have not found such great faith, no, not in Israel."* Those who were sent, returning to the house, found that the servant who had been sick was well.

Soon afterwards, he went to a city called Nain. Many of his disciples, along with a great multitude, went with him. Now when he came near to the gate of the city, behold, one who was dead was carried out, the only son of his mother, and she was a widow. Many people of the city were with her. When the Lord saw her, he had compassion on her, and said to her, *"Don't cry."* He came near and touched the coffin, and the bearers stood still. He said, *"Young man, I tell you, arise!"* He who was dead sat up, and began to speak. And he gave him to his mother.

Fear took hold of all, and they glorified God, saying, "A great prophet has arisen among us!" and, "God has visited his people!" This report went out concerning him in the whole of Judea, and in all the surrounding region.

The disciples of John told him about all these things. John, calling to himself two of his disciples, sent them to Jesus, saying, "Are you the one who is coming, or should we look for another?" When the men had come to him, they said, "John the Baptizer has sent us to you, saying, 'Are you he who comes, or should we look for another?'"

In that hour he cured many of diseases and plagues and evil spirits; and to many who were blind he gave sight. Jesus answered them, *"Go and tell John the things which you have seen and heard: that the blind receive their sight, the lame walk, the lepers are cleansed, the deaf hear, the dead are raised up, and the poor have good news preached to them. Blessed is he who finds no occasion for stumbling in me."*

When John's messengers had departed, he began to tell the multitudes about John, *"What did you go out into the wilderness to see? A reed shaken by the wind? But what did you go out to see? A man clothed in soft clothing? Behold, those who are gorgeously dressed, and live delicately, are in kings' courts. But what did you go out to see? A prophet? Yes, I tell you, and much more than a prophet. This is he of whom it is written, 'Behold, I send my messenger before your face, who will prepare your way before you.'*

"For I tell you, among those who are born of women there is not a greater prophet than John the Baptizer, yet he who is least in God's Kingdom is greater than he."

When all the people and the tax collectors heard this, they declared God to be just, having been baptized with John's baptism. But the Pharisees and the lawyers rejected the counsel of God, not being baptized by him themselves.

"To what then should I compare the people of this generation? What are they like? They are like children who sit in the marketplace, and call to one another, saying, 'We piped to you, and you didn't dance. We mourned, and you didn't weep.' For John the Baptizer came neither eating bread nor drinking wine, and you say, 'He has a demon.' The Son of Man has come eating and drinking, and you say, 'Behold, a gluttonous man, and a drunkard; a friend of tax collectors and sinners!' Wisdom is justified by all her children."

One of the Pharisees invited him to eat with him. He entered into the Pharisee's house, and sat at the table. Behold, a woman in the city who was a sinner, when she knew that he was reclining in the Pharisee's house, brought an alabaster jar of ointment. Standing behind at his feet weeping, she began to wet his feet with her tears, and she wiped them with the hair of her head, kissed his feet, and anointed them with the ointment.

Now when the Pharisee who had invited him saw it, he said to himself, "This man, if he were a prophet, would have perceived who and what kind of woman this is who touches him, that she is a sinner."

Jesus answered him, *"Simon, I have something to tell you."*

He said, "Teacher, say on."

"A certain lender had two debtors. The one owed five hundred denarii, and the other fifty. When they couldn't pay, he forgave them both. Which of them therefore will love him most?"

Simon answered, "He, I suppose, to whom he forgave the most."

He said to him, *"You have judged correctly."* Turning to the woman, he said to Simon, *"Do you see this woman? I entered into your house, and you gave me no water for my feet, but she has wet my feet with her tears, and wiped them with the hair of her head. You gave me no kiss, but she, since the time I came in, has not ceased to kiss my feet. You didn't anoint my head with oil, but she has anointed my feet with ointment. Therefore I tell you, her sins, which are many, are forgiven, for she loved much. But one to whom little is forgiven, loves little."* He said to her, *"Your sins are forgiven."*

Those who sat at the table with him began to say to themselves, "Who is this who even forgives sins?"

He said to the woman, *"Your faith has saved you. Go in peace."*

ARCHAEOLOGICAL AND HISTORICAL EVIDENCE:

We discussed Capernaum in Chapter 4's notes, so we won't cover evidence for Capernaum again.

In the 1st century B.C., the Roman army consisted of cohorts with six 100-man legions. Each legion had ten cohorts led by individual centurions, so the number of centurions in a cohort was 60. Polybius wrote about the structure of the Roman legion's in the 2nd century B.C., so documentation states that leaders called centurions existed from before Jesus's life on earth (7.3).

Nain is an Arab village in northern Israel, located in Galilee, about 8 miles south of Nazareth. "The Roman Village of Naim (Nain) was inhabited from the Middle Bronze period, according to survey of ceramics in the graves around the village. It was probably a continuation of the earlier site in Tell Agol during the Hellenistic period (332-37 B.C.). The village reached its peak in the Roman and Byzantine periods (37B.C.-640 A.D.). According to some ancient texts, the Roman village was surrounded by walls. The ruins of the ancient village lay under the new village, in the area of the new Church (which was built in 1880)" (7.1).

Records from 380 A.D. indicate the Widow's house in Nain became a church there, and the village of Nain stands today. In 1880, the ruins of an ancient Church in the village were rebuilt. It contains paintings depicting the resurrection of the Widow's son (7.2).

We discussed archaeological evidence of John the Baptist in Chapter 3 (3.4), and we covered the

Pharisees in Chapter 5 (5.2 & 5.3). As far as I can find, we don't have any additional evidence for Simon, the Pharisee who invited Jesus to dinner, other than what is stated in the books bound together in the Bible.

WHAT DO YOU THINK?

➢ Archaeology confirms the biblical description of the synagogue and Peter's home in Capernaum. In what ways, if any, do the specific, verified archaeological finds we've learned about affect your beliefs about Jesus and the Bible?

_____
_____
_____
_____
_____
_____
_____
_____

➢ Why do you think the Widow's house in Nain was converted to a church within the first century (approximately) after Jesus died? Why do you think the house's conversion into a church was made?

_____
_____
_____
_____
_____
_____
_____
_____

➢ Why would people be full of fear in response to Jesus bringing the young man back to life? What other types of reactions would you expect from eye-witnesses of this event?

_____
_____
_____
_____
_____
_____
_____
_____

➢ Prophecies in Isaiah 29 and 35, written hundreds of years before Jesus lived, told of a Messiah who would restore hearing, restore the sight, heal people, and raise the dead. Isaiah 40:3 and Malachi 3:1 also prophesy about John the Baptist. In what ways do ancient prophecies, written hundreds of years beforehand, act as supporting documentation for events which occurred during Jesus's lifetime?

___

➢ Why do you think John to asked Jesus if He is the Messiah, the one who was prophesied?

___

➢ The Pharisees were key leaders of the community in Jesus's day and they were the main opponents against Jesus. It was clear the Pharisees thought Jesus should avoid the "wrong" sorts of people, like the woman who cleaned his feet and anointed him with oil. Jesus had different views. Based on what you know about Jesus so far, with what sorts of people do you think Jesus wanted to spend time?

___

CHAPTER 8

Soon afterwards, he went about through cities and villages, preaching and bringing the good news of God's Kingdom. With him were the twelve, and certain women who had been healed of evil spirits and infirmities: Mary who was called Magdalene, from whom seven demons had gone out; and Joanna, the wife of Chuza, Herod's steward; Susanna; and many others; who served them from their possessions.

When a great multitude came together, and people from every city were coming to him, he spoke by a parable. *"The farmer went out to sow his seed. As he sowed, some fell along the road, and it was trampled underfoot, and the birds of the sky devoured it. Other seed fell on the rock, and as soon as it grew, it withered away, because it had no moisture. Other fell amid the thorns, and the thorns grew with it, and choked it. Other fell into the good ground, and grew, and produced one hundred times as much fruit."* As he said these things, he called out, *"He who has ears to hear, let him hear!"*

Then his disciples asked him, "What does this parable mean?"

He said, *"To you it is given to know the mysteries of God's Kingdom, but to the rest in parables; that 'seeing they may not see, and hearing they may not understand.' Now the parable is this: The seed is the word of God. Those along the road are those who hear, then the devil comes, and takes away the word from their heart, that they may not believe and be saved. Those on the rock are they who, when they hear, receive the word with joy; but these have no root, who believe for a while, then fall away in time of temptation. That which fell among the thorns, these are those who have heard, and as they go on their way they are choked with cares, riches, and pleasures of life, and bring no fruit to maturity. Those in the good ground, these are those who with an honest and good heart, having heard the word, hold it tightly, and produce fruit with perseverance.*

"No one, when he has lit a lamp, covers it with a container, or puts it under a bed; but puts it on a stand, that those who enter in may see the light. For nothing is hidden that will not be revealed; nor anything secret that will not be known and come to light. Be careful therefore how you hear. For whoever has, to him will be given; and whoever doesn't have, from him will be taken away even that which he thinks he has."

His mother and brothers came to him, and they could not come near him for the crowd. Some people told him, "Your mother and your brothers stand outside, desiring to see you."

But he answered them, *"My mother and my brothers are these who hear the word of God, and do it."*

Now on one of those days, he entered into a boat, himself and his disciples, and he said to them, *"Let's go over to the other side of the lake."* So they launched out. But as they sailed, he fell asleep. A wind storm came down on the lake, and they were taking on dangerous amounts of water. They came to him, and awoke him, saying, "Master, master, we are dying!" He awoke, and rebuked the wind and the raging of the water, and they ceased, and it was calm. He said to them, *"Where is your faith?"* Being afraid they marveled, saying to one another, "Who is this then, that he commands even the winds and the water, and they obey him?"

They arrived at the country of the Gadarenes, which is opposite Galilee. When Jesus stepped ashore, a certain man out of the city who had demons for a long time met him. He wore no clothes, and didn't live in a house, but in the tombs.

When he saw Jesus, he cried out, and fell down before him, and with a loud voice said, "What do I have to do with you, Jesus, you Son of the Most High God? I beg you, don't torment me!" For Jesus was commanding the unclean spirit to come out of the man. For the unclean spirit had often seized the man. He was kept under guard, and bound with chains and fetters. Breaking the bonds apart, he was driven by the demon into the desert.

Jesus asked him, *"What is your name?"*

He said, "Legion," for many demons had entered into him. They begged him that he would not command them to go into the abyss. Now there was there a herd of many pigs feeding on the mountain, and they begged him that he would allow them to enter into those. Then he allowed them. The demons came out of the man, and entered into the pigs, and the herd rushed down the steep bank into the lake, and were drowned. When those who fed them saw what had happened, they fled and told it in the city and in the country.

People went out to see what had happened. They came to Jesus and found the man from whom the demons had gone out, sitting at Jesus' feet, clothed and in his right mind; and they were afraid. Those who saw it told them how he who had been possessed by demons was healed. All the people of the surrounding country of the Gadarenes asked him to depart from them, for they were very much afraid.

Then he entered into the boat and returned. But the man from whom the demons had gone out begged him that he might go with him, but Jesus sent him away, saying, *"Return to your house, and declare what great things God has done for you."*

He went his way, proclaiming throughout the whole city what great things Jesus had done for him.

When Jesus returned, the multitude welcomed him, for they were all waiting for him. Behold, a man named Jairus came. He was a ruler of the synagogue. He fell down at Jesus' feet, and begged him to come into his house, for he had an only daughter, about twelve years of age, and she was dying. But as he went, the multitudes pressed against him. A woman who had a flow of blood for twelve years, who had spent all her living on physicians and could not be healed by any came behind him, and touched the fringe of his cloak. Immediately the flow of her blood stopped. Jesus said, *"Who touched me?"*

When all denied it, Peter and those with him said, "Master, the multitudes press and jostle you, and you say, 'Who touched me?'"

But Jesus said, *"Someone did touch me, for I perceived that power has gone out of me."*

When the woman saw that she was not hidden, she came trembling, and falling down before him declared to him in the presence of all the people the reason why she had touched him, and how she was healed immediately. He said to her, *"Daughter, cheer up. Your faith has made you well. Go in peace."*

While he still spoke, one from the ruler of the synagogue's house came, saying to him, "Your daughter is dead. Don't trouble the Teacher."

But Jesus hearing it, answered him, *"Don't be afraid. Only believe, and she will be healed."*

When he came to the house, he didn't allow anyone to enter in, except Peter, John, James, the father of the child, and her mother. All were weeping and mourning her, but he said, *"Don't weep. She isn't dead, but sleeping."*

They were ridiculing him, knowing that she was dead. But he put them all outside, and taking her by the hand, he called, saying, *"Child, arise!"* Her spirit returned, and she rose up immediately. He commanded that something be given to her to eat. Her parents were amazed, but he commanded them to tell no one what had been done.

ARCHAEOLOGICAL AND HISTORICAL EVIDENCE:

In Luke 8, it says Jesus went about through cities and villages preaching and bringing the good news of God's kingdom, and that people from every city were coming to him. There were many cities and villages in the Galilee region including Sepphoris, Tiberias, Tyre, Ptolemais, Caesarea Philippi, Bethsaida, Scythopolis, Nazareth, and clusters of villages numbering more than 100 (8.1).

Jesus did not travel alone. In this chapter we also have a specific list of people that traveled with Jesus. His companions include the 12 disciples, Mary, Joanna, Susanna, and many others. We've covered the disciples previously, so we will only cover the additionally named women here.

Joanna, wife of Chuza, and Chuza, are individuals for which we have no direct evidence in the archaeological record. The only historical documentation mentioning them is contained in the Bible.

There is "an ossuary outside Jerusalem which houses hundreds of stone coffins of women from the time of Jesus. Helen Bond, an explorer, squeezed through the entry to a tomb dedicated to Jesus's disciple, Salome. Ancient graffiti scratched on the ceiling was dedicated to Salome's healing powers" (8.7). Salome (in the Gospel of Mark) is the same person as Susanna (in the Gospel of Luke). Thus, we have a tomb related to Susanna, who traveled with Jesus.

Mary Magdalene was "always called Mary the Magdalene, never Mary from Magdala, so it (the name Magdalene) wasn't just about where she came from it was also about who she was" (8.7). "A Catholic priest and archaeologists in Israel are excavating an ancient synagogue and a site that may have been the home of Mary Magdalene, who has been called Jesus' most beloved disciple" (8.6). "This may have been home to one of the most important figures of the Bible, Mary Magdalene. The first recorded witness of the resurrection. 'This is a holy site. I am sure of that,' said Father Juan Solana" (8.6). The site of the home dates to Jesus's lifetime, and is another site preserved by Jesus's followers. Again, ask yourself why people would preserve Mary the Magdalene's home site if Jesus wasn't real.

Gadarenes refers to a region on the eastern side of the Sea of Galilee. It was a region inhabited by Gentiles or pagans. There were two known cities in the region, Gerasa and Gadara. Both of these cities are verified archaeologically and in ancient documents (8.2).

There is one steep bank in the region, which is believed to be the specific location for the miracle documented in Luke 8. Luke's narrative describes Jesus going across the sea of Galilee, from the region of Galilee, to an area where there is a bank the swine ran down into the sea. Because there is a bank on the shore of the lake opposite the region of Galilee, geographically we know the description of the area is accurate in Luke's narrative. We have a verified location where the events are likely to have taken place. Therefore, there is no conflict in the description of crossing the lake and reaching a city with a steep bank into the water.

WHAT DO YOU THINK?

➤ In this chapter, Jesus travels further from Galilee, and multitudes continue to follow Him. What are some likely ways in which the news about Jesus and His miracles reached the ears of people in the regions across the Sea of Galilee?

_____
_____
_____
_____
_____
_____
_____
_____
_____

➤ With multitudes following Jesus, why would it be likely for some people to write down their knowledge of and experiences with Jesus? What do you think they would write about Him?

_____
_____
_____
_____
_____
_____
_____
_____
_____

➤ Eight or nine different people wrote the books bound together as the New Testament in the Bible (8.3). Secular people wrote about Jesus too (see reference 8.4). What do you think motivated people to write a lot about Jesus? Would people write so much about Jesus if He wasn't a real person?

_____
_____
_____
_____
_____
_____
_____
_____
_____

- According to Jesus, three out of four types of hearers of God's Word never become mature Christians. Why do you think so few people become mature Christians?

___

- In ancient documents the Jews refer to Jesus as a magician who led the Jewish people astray (8.4). The gospel accounts refer to Jesus as a miracle worker (8.5). Do you believe Jesus truly worked miracles or did magic tricks to fool people? What makes you answer as you did?

___

- Coldcasechristianity.com/writings/is-there-any-evidence-for-jesus-outside-the-bible/ lists 11 non-Biblical authors who wrote about Jesus. Eight or nine Biblical authors wrote about Jesus and His teachings. Given the number of ancient authors who wrote details about Jesus, how likely do you think it is Jesus was a just fictional character versus a real man who lived?

___

CHAPTER 9

He called the twelve together, and gave them power and authority over all demons, and to cure diseases. He sent them out to preach God's Kingdom and to heal the sick. He said to them, *"Take nothing for your journey—no staffs, nor wallet, nor bread, nor money. Don't have two coats each. Into whatever house you enter, stay there, and depart from there. As many as don't receive you, when you depart from that city, shake off even the dust from your feet for a testimony against them."*

They departed and went throughout the villages, preaching the Good News and healing everywhere. Now Herod the tetrarch heard of all that was done by him; and he was very perplexed, because it was said by some that John had risen from the dead, and by some that Elijah had appeared, and by others that one of the old prophets had risen again. Herod said, "I beheaded John, but who is this about whom I hear such things?" He sought to see him.

The apostles, when they had returned, told him what things they had done.

He took them and withdrew apart to a desert

region of a city called Bethsaida. But the multitudes, perceiving it, followed him. He welcomed them, spoke to them of God's Kingdom, and he cured those who needed healing. The day began to wear away; and the twelve came and said to him, "Send the multitude away, that they may go into the surrounding villages and farms, and lodge, and get food, for we are here in a deserted place."

But he said to them, *"You give them something to eat."*

They said, "We have no more than five loaves and two fish, unless we should go and buy food for all these people." For they were about five thousand men.

He said to his disciples, *"Make them sit down in groups of about fifty each."* They did so, and made them all sit down. He took the five loaves and the two fish, and looking up to the sky, he blessed them, broke them, and gave them to the disciples to set before the multitude. They ate and were all filled. They gathered up twelve baskets of broken pieces that were left over.

As he was praying alone, the disciples were with him, and he asked them, *"Who do the multitudes say that I am?"*

They answered, "'John the Baptizer,' but others say, 'Elijah,' and others, that one of the old prophets has risen again."

He said to them, *"But who do you say that I am?"*

Peter answered, "The Christ of God."

But he warned them, and commanded them to tell this to no one, saying, *"The Son of Man must suffer many things, and be rejected by the elders, chief priests, and scribes, and be killed, and the third day be raised up."*

He said to all, *"If anyone desires to come after me, let him deny himself, take up his cross, and follow me. For whoever desires to save his life will lose it, but whoever will lose his life for my sake, will save it. For what does it profit a man if he gains the whole world, and loses or forfeits his own self? For whoever will be ashamed of me and of my words, of him will the Son of Man be ashamed, when he comes in his glory, and the glory of the Father, and of the holy angels. But I tell you the truth: There are some of those who stand here who will in no way taste of death until they see God's Kingdom."*

About eight days after these sayings, he took with him Peter, John, and James, and went up onto the mountain to pray. As he was praying, the appearance of his face was altered, and his clothing became white and dazzling. Behold, two men were talking with him, who were Moses and Elijah, who appeared in glory, and spoke of his departure, which he was about to accomplish at Jerusalem.

Now Peter and those who were with him were heavy with sleep, but when they were fully awake, they saw his glory, and the two men who stood with him. As they were parting from him, Peter said to Jesus, "Master, it is good for us to be here. Let's make three tents: one for you, one for Moses, and one for Elijah," not knowing what he said.

While he said these things, a cloud came and over-shadowed them, and they were afraid as they entered into the cloud. A voice came out of the cloud, saying, *"This is my beloved Son. Listen to him!"* When the voice came, Jesus was found alone. They were silent, and told no one in those days any of the things which they had seen.

On the next day, when they had come down from the mountain, a great multitude met him. Behold, a man from the crowd called out, saying, "Teacher, I beg you to look at my son, for he is my only child. Behold, a spirit takes him, he suddenly cries out, and it convulses him so that he foams, and it hardly departs from him, bruising him severely. I begged your disciples to cast it out, and they couldn't."

Jesus answered, *"Faithless and perverse generation, how long shall I be with you and bear with you? Bring your son here."*

While he was still coming, the demon threw him down and convulsed him violently. But Jesus rebuked the unclean spirit, healed the boy, and gave him back to his father. They were all astonished at the majesty of God.

But while all were marveling at all the things which Jesus did, he said to his disciples, *"Let these words sink into your ears, for the Son of Man will be delivered up into the hands of men."* But they didn't understand this saying. It was concealed from them, that they should not perceive it, and they were afraid to ask him about this saying.

An argument arose among them about which of them was the greatest. Jesus, perceiving the reasoning of their hearts, took a little child, and set him by his side, and said to them, *"Whoever receives this little child in my name receives me. Whoever receives me receives him who sent me. For whoever is least among you all, this one will be great."*

John answered, "Master, we saw someone casting out demons in your name, and we forbade him, because he doesn't follow with us."

Jesus said to him, *"Don't forbid him, for he who is not against us is for us."*

It came to pass, when the days were near that he should be taken up, he intently set his face to go to Jerusalem and sent messengers before his face. They went and entered into a village of the Samaritans, so as to prepare for him. They didn't receive him, because he was traveling with his face set toward Jerusalem. When his disciples, James and John, saw this, they said, "Lord, do you want us to command fire to come down from the sky, and destroy them, just as Elijah did?"

But he turned and rebuked them, *"You don't know of what kind of spirit you are. For the Son of Man didn't come to destroy men's lives, but to save them."*

They went to another village. As they went on the way, a certain man said to him, "I want to follow you wherever you go, Lord."

Jesus said to him, *"The foxes have holes, and the birds of the sky have nests, but the Son of Man has no place to lay his head."*

He said to another, *"Follow me!"*

But he said, "Lord, allow me first to go and bury my father."

But Jesus said to him, *"Leave the dead to bury their own dead, but you go and announce God's Kingdom."*

Another also said, "I want to follow you, Lord, but first allow me to say good-bye to those who are at my house."

But Jesus said to him, *"No one, having put his hand to the plow, and looking back, is fit for God's Kingdom."*

ARCHAEOLOGICAL AND HISTORICAL EVIDENCE:

Bethsaida has been the site of archaeological expeditions since 1995, ongoing. The Bethsaida Excavation Project has yielded city walls, towers, coins, a tunnel, paved roadway, building structures, city gates, and more. BethsaidaArchaeology.org provides a wealth of information about this specific city, as well as insights about life in the region, artifacts of all kinds, and the revelation of building structures (9.1).

Additionally, archaeological excavations are proving to be in line with both biblical and secular historic descriptions written about the village. Although there is some debate as to whether the current site being excavated is actually the ancient city of Bethsaida, there is no variation in the evidence yet which indicates it is anything other than Bethsaida.

In this chapter of Luke, we see that Jesus set his face to go to Jerusalem. Jerusalem has existed for more than three thousand years in definitive history, and quite possibly much earlier with archaeologists debating finds from as far back as about 5000 B.C. Jerusalem is listed as one of the oldest cities on Earth. Artifacts found in Jerusalem provide the oldest ancient Hebrew Biblical text ever found, the earliest mention of Bethlehem, and independent evidence that the city of Bethlehem was in the Kingdom of Judah.

Jerusalem is mentioned in the Bible 810 times, and is first mentioned in relation to Abraham in Genesis 14. One could say that Jerusalem is a key city in the narrative of the Bible, which yields more archaeological evidence for the truth of the Bible than just about any other location on earth. See resources listed at reference 9.2 for more information about Jerusalem.

WHAT DO YOU THINK?

➢ What do you think compelled Jesus to focus on reaching as many people as possible, with the Good News about our ability to have forgiveness for our sins through Him, during His short lifetime?

___

➢ What makes people, throughout time, continually speculate about who Jesus really is rather than accepting who Jesus said He is?

___

➢ What are your beliefs about the transfiguration event where Jesus became dazzling white, appeared with Moses and Elijah, and God spoke in an audible voice? If people believe Jesus is God's Son as He says He is, is this supernatural event plausible? Why or why not?

___

➢ Jesus "set His face to go to Jerusalem," knowing He would be tortured and killed there. What insights about Jesus's character and mission do you see in His determination?

➢ If Jesus didn't come to destroy lives, but came to save them, why do you think so many people destroy other people's lives in the name of their religion? (Consider all religions, but especially those who kill Christians, as well as Christians who've killed people of other religions.)

➢ Why does it matter what you, or anyone else, thinks about Jesus?

CHAPTER 10

Now after these things, the Lord also appointed seventy others, and sent them two by two ahead of him into every city and place where he was about to come.

Then he said to them, *"The harvest is indeed plentiful, but the laborers are few. Pray therefore to the Lord of the harvest, that he may send out laborers into his harvest. Go your ways. Behold, I send you out as lambs among wolves. Carry no purse, nor wallet, nor sandals. Greet no one on the way. Into whatever house you enter, first say, 'Peace be to this house.' If a son of peace is there, your peace will rest on him; but if not, it will return to you. Remain in that same house, eating and drinking the things they give, for the laborer is worthy of his wages.*

"Don't go from house to house. Into whatever city you enter, and they receive you, eat the things that are set before you. Heal the sick who are there, and tell them, 'God's Kingdom has come near to you.' But into whatever city you enter, and they don't receive you, go out into its streets and say, 'Even the dust from your city that clings to us, we wipe off against you. Nevertheless know

this, that God's Kingdom has come near to you.' I tell you, it will be more tolerable in that day for Sodom than for that city.

"Woe to you, Chorazin! Woe to you, Bethsaida! For if the mighty works had been done in Tyre and Sidon which were done in you, they would have repented long ago, sitting in sackcloth and ashes. But it will be more tolerable for Tyre and Sidon in the judgment than for you. You, Capernaum, who are exalted to heaven, will be brought down to Hades. Whoever listens to you listens to me, and whoever rejects you rejects me. Whoever rejects me rejects him who sent me."

The seventy returned with joy, saying, "Lord, even the demons are subject to us in your name!"

He said to them, *"I saw Satan having fallen like lightning from heaven. Behold, I give you authority to tread on serpents and scorpions, and over all the power of the enemy. Nothing will in any way hurt you. Nevertheless, don't rejoice in this, that the spirits are subject to you, but rejoice that your names are written in heaven."*

In that same hour Jesus rejoiced in the Holy Spirit, and said, *"I thank you, O Father, Lord of heaven and earth, that you have hidden these things from the wise and understanding, and revealed them to little children. Yes, Father, for so it was well-pleasing in your sight."*

Turning to the disciples, he said, *"All things have been delivered to me by my Father. No one knows who the Son is, except the Father, and who the Father is, except the Son, and he to whomever the Son desires to reveal him."*

Turning to the disciples, he said privately, *"Blessed are the eyes which see the things that you see, for I tell you that many prophets and kings desired to see the things which you see, and didn't see them, and to hear the things which you hear, and didn't hear them."*

Behold, a certain lawyer stood up and tested him, saying, "Teacher, what shall I do to inherit eternal life?"

He said to him, *"What is written in the law? How do you read it?"*

He answered, "You shall love the Lord your God with all your heart, with all your soul, with all your strength, and with all your mind; and your neighbor as yourself."

He said to him, *"You have answered correctly. Do this, and you will live."*

But he, desiring to justify himself, asked Jesus, "Who is my neighbor?"

Jesus answered, *"A certain man was going down from Jerusalem to Jericho, and he fell among robbers, who both stripped him and beat him, and departed, leaving him half dead. By chance a certain priest was going down that way. When he saw him, he passed by on the other side. In the same way a Levite also, when he came to the place, and saw him, passed by on the other side.*

"But a certain Samaritan, as he traveled, came where he was. When he saw him, he was moved with compassion, came to him, and bound up his wounds, pouring on oil and wine. He set him on his own animal, brought him to an inn, and took care of him. On the next day, when he departed, he took out two denarii, gave them to the host, and said to him, 'Take care of him. Whatever you spend beyond that, I will repay you when I return.' Now which of these three do you think seemed to be a neighbor to him who fell among the robbers?"

He said, "He who showed mercy on him."

Then Jesus said to him, *"Go and do likewise."*

As they went on their way, he entered into a certain village, and a certain woman named Martha received him into her house. She had a sister called Mary, who also sat at Jesus' feet, and heard his word. But Martha was distracted with much serving, and she came up to him, and said, "Lord, don't you care that my sister left me to serve alone? Ask her therefore to help me."

Jesus answered her, *"Martha, Martha, you are anxious and troubled about many things, but one thing is needed. Mary has chosen the good part, which will not be taken away from her."*

ARCHAEOLOGICAL AND HISTORICAL EVIDENCE:

There are seven ancient cities mentioned in this chapter, which we previously explored. They are: Chorazin, Bethsaida, Tyre, Sidon, Capernaum, Jerusalem, and Jericho, which are all verified cities documented in archaeological finds or ancient documents outside of the Bible. Jerusalem and Jericho are still active, inhabited cities today. As archaeological digs explore increasing numbers of areas involved in biblical history, confirmation of the reality of places, practices, and people continues grow.

WHAT DO YOU THINK?

➤ Jesus sent 35 teams of two disciples each ahead of Him into the places He was traveling. In what ways was this an effective strategy for Jesus to maximize the sharing of his Good News?

➤ Jesus said "*Woe to you, Chorazin! Woe to you, Bethsaida!*" Both of those cities are now archaeological ruins (10.1). What cities, regions, or countries do you think Jesus would issue woe statements toward today? Why?

➢ With what you have read in this Gospel of Luke so far, who do you think the people are from which God's knowledge is hidden? Why would God hide his knowledge and understanding from people who think of themselves as wiser than everyone else?

➢ What roles do open-mindedness, close-mindedness, and wisdom have in a person's willingness to explore whether Jesus is real and to consider whether a spiritual realm really exists?

➢ Why do you think some people don't see, hear, or understand spiritual things?

➤ The two greatest Commandments in the Bible are to love the Lord God with all of our heart, soul, strength and mind, and to love our neighbors as ourselves. What makes it so hard for all of us to truly obey these two simple, straightforward directives from God?

CHAPTER 11

When he finished praying in a certain place, one of his disciples said to him, "Lord, teach us to pray, just as John also taught his disciples."

He said to them, *"When you pray, say,*

'Our Father which art in heaven, Hallowed be thy name.

Thy kingdom come. Thy will be done, on earth as it is in heaven.

Give us day by day our daily bread.

And forgive us our sins; for we forgive those who sin against us.

And lead us not into temptation; but deliver us from the evil one.'"

He said to them, *"Which of you, if you go to a friend at midnight, and tell him, 'Friend, lend me three loaves of bread, for a friend of mine has come to me from a journey, and I have nothing to set before him,' and he from within will answer and say, 'Don't bother me. The door is now shut, and my children are with me in bed. I can't get up and give it to you'? I tell you, although he will not rise and give it to him because he is his friend, yet because of his persistence, he will get up and give him as many as he needs.*

"I tell you, keep asking, and it will be given you. Keep seeking, and you will find. Keep knocking, and it will be opened to you. For everyone who asks receives. He who seeks finds. To him who knocks it will be opened.

"Which of you fathers, if your son asks for bread, will give him a stone? Or if he asks for a fish, he won't give him a snake instead of a fish, will he? Or if he asks for an egg, he won't give him a scorpion, will he? If you then, being evil, know how to give good gifts to your children, how much more will your heavenly Father give the Holy Spirit to those who ask him?"

He was casting out a demon, and it was mute. When the demon had gone out, the mute man spoke; and the multitudes marveled. But some of them said, "He casts out demons by Beelzebul, the prince of the demons." Others, testing him, sought from him a sign from heaven.

But he, knowing their thoughts, said to them, "Every kingdom divided against itself is brought to desolation. A house divided against itself falls. If Satan also is divided against himself, how will his kingdom stand? For you say that I cast out demons by Beelzebul. But if I cast out demons by Beelzebul, by whom do your children cast them out? Therefore they will be your judges. But if I by God's finger cast out demons, then God's Kingdom has come to you.

"When the strong man, fully armed, guards his own dwelling, his goods are safe. But when someone stronger attacks him and overcomes him, he takes from him his whole armor in which he trusted, and divides his plunder.

"He that is not with me is against me. He who doesn't gather with me scatters. The unclean spirit, when he has gone out of the man, passes through dry places, seeking rest, and finding none, he says, 'I will turn back to my house from which I came out.' When he returns, he finds it swept and put in order. Then he goes, and takes seven other spirits more evil than himself, and they enter in and dwell there. The last state of that man becomes worse than the first."

It came to pass, as he said these things, a certain woman out of the multitude lifted up her voice, and said to him, "Blessed is the womb that bore you, and the breasts which nursed you!"

But he said, *"On the contrary, blessed are those who hear the word of God, and keep it."*

When the multitudes were gathering together to him, he began to say, *"This is an evil generation. It seeks after a sign. No sign will be given to it but the sign of Jonah, the prophet. For even as Jonah became a sign to the Ninevites, so the Son of Man will also be to this generation. The Queen of the South will rise up in the judgment with the men of this generation, and will condemn them: for she came from the ends of the earth to hear the wisdom of Solomon; and behold, one greater than Solomon is here. The men of Nineveh will stand up in the judgment with this generation, and will condemn it: for they repented at the preaching of Jonah, and behold, one greater than Jonah is here.*

"No one, when he has lit a lamp, puts it in a cellar or under a basket, but on a stand, that those who come in may see the light. The lamp of the body is the eye. Therefore when your eye is good, your whole body is also full of light; but when it is evil, your body also is full of darkness. Therefore see whether the light that is in you isn't darkness. If therefore your whole body is full of light, having no part dark, it will be wholly full of light, as when the lamp with its bright shining gives you light."

Now as he spoke, a certain Pharisee asked him to dine with him. He went in, and sat at the table. When the Pharisee saw it, he marveled that he had not first washed himself before dinner. The Lord said to him, *"Now you Pharisees cleanse the outside of the cup and of the platter, but your inward part is full of extortion and wickedness. You foolish ones, didn't he who made the outside make the inside also? But give for gifts to the needy those things which are within, and behold, all things will be clean to you. But woe to you Pharisees! For you tithe mint and rue and every herb, but you bypass justice and God's love. You ought to have done these, and not to have left the other undone. Woe to you Pharisees! For you love the best seats in the synagogues, and the greetings in the marketplaces. Woe to you, scribes and Pharisees, hypocrites! For you are like hidden graves, and the men who walk over them don't know it."*

One of the lawyers answered him, "Teacher, in saying this you insult us also."

He said, *"Woe to you lawyers also! For you load men with burdens that are difficult to carry, and you yourselves won't even lift one finger to help carry those burdens. Woe to you! For you build the tombs of the prophets, and your fathers killed them. So you testify and consent to the works of your fathers. For they killed them, and you build their tombs. Therefore also the wisdom of God said, 'I will send to them prophets and apostles; and some of them they will kill and persecute, that the blood of all the prophets, which was shed from the foundation of the world, may be required of this generation; from the blood of Abel to the blood of Zachariah, who perished between the altar and the sanctuary.' Yes, I tell you, it will be required of this generation. Woe to you lawyers! For you took away the key of knowledge. You didn't enter in yourselves, and those who were entering in, you hindered."*

As he said these things to them, the scribes and the Pharisees began to be terribly angry, and to draw many things out of him; lying in wait for him, and seeking to catch him in something he might say, that they might accuse him.

ARCHAEOLOGICAL AND HISTORICAL EVIDENCE:

This chapter contains Jesus's teachings, so we don't have new characters, places, or practices to investigate historically or archaeologically in this chapter.

WHAT DO YOU THINK?

➤ What, if anything, do you find unusual about the way Jesus teaches and responds to questions?

➤ Why do you think Jesus's teachings have continually influenced world culture for more than 2,000 years? To what would you attribute Jesus's ongoing influence?

➤ Why do you think many people find it difficult to pray?

➤ If Jesus was just a crazy man who had the spirit of a demon, what long-term affect would you expect Him to have on society and in the world more than 2000 years later?

➤ Jesus said, "Blessed are those who hear the word of God, and keep it." Which commands that Jesus taught would we be wise for people to continue obeying today?

➤ Every generation wants more proof of God. Why do you think God puts the responsibility on us to seek God, to ask Him for wisdom and the Holy Spirit, rather than God continually working to prove Himself plainly to all people who question His existence?

➤ Everyone carries an ideal vision of who they should be and who others should be, when it comes to individual goodness and righteousness. How do our ideals make every one of us a hypocrite?

➤ What expectations from others are burdensome to you? How are your expectations of others a burden to them?

➢ In what ways do lawyers and those who file lawsuits lay unreasonable burdens on others, which the lawyers and lawsuit filers wouldn't want to carry themselves?

_____
_____
_____
_____
_____
_____
_____
_____

➢ Why do you think Jesus still has a lasting impact on the world and numerous followers, even though he offended large numbers of officials, leaders, lawyers, rich people, etc. with His teachings about their greed, burdens, wickedness, and self-centered practices?

_____
_____
_____
_____
_____
_____
_____
_____

CHAPTER 12

Meanwhile, when a multitude of many thousands had gathered together, so much so that they trampled on each other, he began to tell his disciples first of all, *"Beware of the yeast of the Pharisees, which is hypocrisy. But there is nothing covered up that will not be revealed, nor hidden that will not be known. Therefore whatever you have said in the darkness will be heard in the light. What you have spoken in the ear in the inner rooms will be proclaimed on the housetops.*

"I tell you, my friends, don't be afraid of those who kill the body, and after that have no more that they can do. But I will warn you whom you should fear. Fear him who after he has killed, has power to cast into Gehenna. Yes, I tell you, fear him.

"Aren't five sparrows sold for two assaria coins? Not one of them is forgotten by God. But the very hairs of your head are all counted. Therefore don't be afraid. You are of more value than many sparrows.

"I tell you, everyone who confesses me before men, the Son of Man will also confess before the angels of God; but he who denies

me in the presence of men will be denied in the presence of God's angels. Everyone who speaks a word against the Son of Man will be forgiven, but those who blaspheme against the Holy Spirit will not be forgiven. When they bring you before the synagogues, the rulers, and the authorities, don't be anxious how or what you will answer, or what you will say; for the Holy Spirit will teach you in that same hour what you must say."

One of the multitude said to him, "Teacher, tell my brother to divide the inheritance with me."

But he said to him, "Man, who made me a judge or an arbitrator over you?" He said to them, "Beware! Keep yourselves from covetousness, for a man's life doesn't consist of the abundance of the things which he possesses."

He spoke a parable to them, saying, "The ground of a certain rich man produced abundantly. He reasoned within himself, saying, 'What will I do, because I don't have room to store my crops?' He said, 'This is what I will do. I will pull down my barns, build bigger ones, and there I will store all my grain and my goods. I will tell my soul, "Soul, you have many goods laid up for many years. Take your ease, eat, drink, and be merry."'

"But God said to him, 'You foolish one, tonight your soul is required of you. The things which you have prepared—whose will they be?' So is he who lays up treasure for himself, and is not rich toward God."

He said to his disciples, "Therefore I tell you, don't be anxious for your life, what you will eat, nor yet for your body, what you will wear. Life is more than food, and the body is more than clothing. Consider the ravens: they don't sow, they don't reap, they have no warehouse or barn, and God feeds them. How much more valuable are you than birds! Which of you by being anxious can add a cubit to his height?

"If then you aren't able to do even the least things, why are you anxious about the rest? Consider the lilies, how they grow. They don't toil, neither do they spin; yet I tell you, even Solomon in all his glory was not arrayed like one of these. But if this is how God clothes the grass in the field, which today exists, and tomorrow is cast into the oven, how much more will he clothe you, O you of little faith? Don't seek what you will eat or what you will drink; neither be anxious. For the nations of the world seek after all of these things, but your Father knows that you need these things. But seek God's Kingdom, and all these things will be added to you. Don't be afraid, little flock, for it is your Father's good pleasure to give you the Kingdom. Sell that which you have, and give gifts to the needy. Make for yourselves purses which don't grow old, a treasure in the heavens that doesn't fail, where no thief approaches, neither moth destroys. For where your treasure is, there will your heart be also.

"Let your waist be dressed and your lamps burning. Be like men watching for their lord, when he returns from the wedding feast; that when he comes and knocks, they may immediately open to him. Blessed are those servants, whom the lord will find watching when he comes. Most certainly I tell you that he will dress himself, make them recline, and will come and serve them. They will be blessed if he comes in the second or third watch, and finds them so. But know this, that if the master of the house had known in what hour the thief was coming, he would have watched, and not allowed his house to be broken into. Therefore be ready also, for the Son of Man is coming in an hour that you don't expect him."

Peter said to him, "Lord, are you telling this parable to us, or to everybody?"

The Lord said, *"Who then is the faithful and wise steward, whom his lord will set over* his household, to give them their portion of food at the right times? Blessed is that servant whom his lord will find doing so when he comes. Truly I tell you, that he will set him over all that he has. But if that servant says in his heart, 'My lord delays his coming,' and begins to beat the menservants and the maidservants, and to eat and drink, and to be drunken, then the lord of that servant will come in a day when he isn't expecting him, and in an hour that he doesn't know, and will cut him in two, and place his portion with the unfaithful. That servant, who knew his lord's will, and didn't prepare, nor do what he wanted, will be beaten with many stripes, but he who didn't know, and did things worthy of stripes, will be beaten with few stripes. To whomever much is given, of him will much be required; and to whom much was entrusted, of him more will be asked.

"I came to throw fire on the earth. I wish it were already kindled. But I have a baptism to be baptized with, and how distressed I am until it is accomplished! Do you think that I have come to give peace in the earth? I tell you, no, but rather division. For from now on, there will be five in one house divided, three against two, and two against three. They will be divided, father against son, and son against father; mother against daughter, and daughter against her mother; mother-in-law against her daughter-in-law, and daughter-in-law against her mother-in-law."

He said to the multitudes also, "When you see a cloud rising from the west, immediately you say, 'A shower is coming,' and so it happens. When a south wind blows, you say, 'There will be a scorching heat,' and it happens. You hypocrites! You know how to interpret the appearance of the earth and the sky, but how is it that you don't interpret this time? Why don't you judge for yourselves what is right? For when you are going with your adversary before the magistrate, try diligently on the *way to be released from him, lest perhaps he drag you to the judge, and the judge deliver you to the officer, and the officer throw you into prison. I tell you, you will by no means get out of there, until you have paid the very last penny."*

ARCHAEOLOGICAL AND HISTORICAL EVIDENCE:

Crowds gathering to see Jesus continually increased in size, as seen in size of the crowd at the feeding of 5000 in chapter 9. In this chapter, Jesus has a multitude of many thousands gathered to hear him speak and to experience his miracles. Jesus had renowned fame in a short span of time. He was well known among the people and influenced many lives.

The key historical figure mentioned in this chapter is Solomon. Evidence from the Temple mount in Jerusalem has provided insights and verification of the civilization surrounding King Solomon, and his father, King David, at the corresponding time in history. "Thousands of coins, stone weights, arrowheads, pottery, mosaic pieces and more show clearly that there was significant human activity at the right time and place to support the existence of David and Solomon's kingdoms" (12.1).

WHAT DO YOU THINK?

➤ There are a number of history books and documents which discuss the kingdoms of King David and King Solomon. What makes people believe these Kings were real, but they think the Bible is fiction?

➤ In the past, what perceptions did you have regarding the number of people following Jesus during His life on Earth? What prevents people from having accurate perceptions about Jesus' life?

- If someone believes there is a God, and believes Jesus is His son, what types of consequences would you expect if they don't spend time seeking God?

- Jesus said He came to bring division on Earth; people will be divided for Him or against Him. What affect do divisions over Jesus have on society today? Why are people still so divided over Jesus?

- Jesus says when He returns He will judge people based on whether they believe Him (have faith in Him) or not. How would you explain your beliefs about Jesus to Him, if he appeared in front of you?

- What do you think makes a person feel valued by God versus ignored by God?

➢ What kinds of treasures can you gather on earth, which are eternal and cannot be stolen?

➢ What characteristics do you think God is looking for in faithful and wise stewards?

CHAPTER 13

Now there were some present at the same time who told him about the Galileans, whose blood Pilate had mixed with their sacrifices. Jesus answered them, *"Do you think that these Galileans were worse sinners than all the other Galileans, because they suffered such things? I tell you, no, but unless you repent, you will all perish in the same way. Or those eighteen, on whom the tower in Siloam fell and killed them; do you think that they were worse offenders than all the men who dwell in Jerusalem? I tell you, no, but, unless you repent, you will all perish in the same way."*

He spoke this parable. *"A certain man had a fig tree planted in his vineyard, and he came seeking fruit on it, and found none. He said to the vine dresser, 'Behold, these three years I have come looking for fruit on this fig tree, and found none. Cut it down. Why does it waste the soil?' He answered, 'Lord, leave it alone this year also, until I dig around it and fertilize it. If it bears fruit, fine; but if not, after that, you can cut it down.'"*

He was teaching in one of the synagogues

on the Sabbath day. Behold, there was a woman who had a spirit of infirmity eighteen years. She was bent over, and could in no way straighten herself up. When Jesus saw her, he called her, and said to her, *"Woman, you are freed from your infirmity."* He laid his hands on her, and immediately she stood up straight and glorified God.

The ruler of the synagogue, being indignant because Jesus had healed on the Sabbath, said to the multitude, "There are six days in which men ought to work. Therefore come on those days and be healed, and not on the Sabbath day!"

Therefore the Lord answered him, *"You hypocrites! Doesn't each one of you free his ox or his donkey from the stall on the Sabbath, and lead him away to water? Ought not this woman, being a daughter of Abraham whom Satan had bound eighteen long years, be freed from this bondage on the Sabbath day?"*

As he said these things, all his adversaries were disappointed and all the multitude rejoiced for all the glorious things that were done by him.

He said, *"What is God's Kingdom like? To what shall I compare it? It is like a grain of mustard seed which a man took and put in his own garden. It grew and became a large tree, and the birds of the sky live in its branches."*

Again he said, *"To what shall I compare God's Kingdom? It is like yeast, which a woman took and hid in three measures of flour, until it was all leavened."*

He went on his way through cities and villages, teaching, and traveling on to Jerusalem. One said to him, "Lord, are they few who are saved?"

He said to them, *"Strive to enter in by the narrow door, for many, I tell you, will seek to enter in and will not be able. When once the master of the house has risen up, and has shut the door, and you begin to stand outside and to knock at the door, saying, 'Lord, Lord, open to us!' then he will answer and tell you, 'I don't know you or where you come from.' Then you will begin to say, 'We ate and drank in your presence, and you taught in our streets.' He will say, 'I tell you, I don't know where you come from. Depart from me, all you workers of iniquity.' There will be weeping and gnashing of teeth when you see Abraham, Isaac, Jacob, and all the prophets in God's Kingdom, and yourselves being thrown outside. They will come from the east, west, north, and south, and will sit down in God's Kingdom. Behold, there are some who are last who will be first, and there are some who are first who will be last."*

On that same day, some Pharisees came, saying to him, "Get out of here, and go away, for Herod wants to kill you."

He said to them, *"Go and tell that fox, 'Behold, I cast out demons and perform cures today and tomorrow, and the third day I complete my mission. Nevertheless I must go on my way today and tomorrow and the next day, for it can't be that a prophet would perish outside of Jerusalem.'*

"Jerusalem, Jerusalem, you who kills the prophets and stones those who are sent to her! How often I wanted to gather your children together, like a hen gathers her own brood under her wings, and you refused! Behold, your house is left to you desolate. I tell you, you will not see me until you say, 'Blessed is he who comes in the name of the Lord!'"

ARCHAEOLOGICAL AND HISTORICAL EVIDENCE:

We previously talked about Galilee, where the Galileans lived, beginning with Chapter 1. Therefore, we won't discuss Galilee again in this chapter.

A new mention in this chapter is the fall of the Tower of Siloam. The remains of a circular footing for the Tower of Siloam have been found. The footing is by a wall that is more than 5000 years old at the city of David (13.1). Even seemingly small events in the Bible can be confirmed, such as the falling of the Tower of Siloam, as archaeologists continue to find Biblical artifacts and make new discoveries.

WHAT DO YOU THINK?

➤ What is the primary difference between Jesus as a religious leader and other religious leaders, like the ruler at the synagogue, the high priests and scribes? Who do you think interprets God's Commandments in the proper Spirit, as God intended, and why do you think that?

_____
_____
_____
_____
_____
_____
_____
_____
_____

➤ The Kingdom of God continues to grow as people throughout the centuries continue to follow Jesus. With all you've learned so far, what would you say the kingdom of God is like?

_____
_____
_____
_____
_____
_____
_____
_____

➤ What do you think Jesus meant when He explained who will be saved, and He said to strive to enter the narrow door?

_____
_____
_____
_____
_____
_____
_____
_____
_____

➢ What kinds of hypocritical things do people do today, whether they are Christian or not?

➢ Jesus said people will come from the east, west, north, and south, and will sit down in God's Kingdom. Today there are Christians all over the world. What has Jesus said about God's kingdom which has proven to be true, so far?

➢ Why did Jesus call Jerusalem the city who "kills prophets and stones those who are sent to her?" Why do you think people in Jerusalem were so intolerant toward the prophets of God?

CHAPTER 14

When he went into the house of one of the rulers of the Pharisees on a Sabbath to eat bread, they were watching him. Behold, a certain man who had dropsy was in front of him. Jesus, answering, spoke to the lawyers and Pharisees, saying, *"Is it lawful to heal on the Sabbath?"*

But they were silent.

He took him, and healed him, and let him go. He answered them, *"Which of you, if your son or an ox fell into a well, wouldn't immediately pull him out on a Sabbath day?"*

They couldn't answer him regarding these things.

He spoke a parable to those who were invited, when he noticed how they chose the best seats, and said to them, *"When you are invited by anyone to a wedding feast, don't sit in the best seat, since perhaps someone more honorable than you might be invited by him, and he who invited both of you would come and tell you, 'Make room for this person.' Then you would begin, with shame, to take the lowest place. But when you are invited, go and sit in the lowest place, so that when he who invited you comes, he may tell you, 'Friend, move up higher.' Then you will be honored in the presence of all who sit at the table with you. For everyone who exalts himself will be humbled, and whoever humbles himself will be exalted."*

He also said to the one who had invited him, *"When you make a dinner or a supper, don't call your friends, nor your brothers, nor your kinsmen, nor rich neighbors, or perhaps they might also return the favor, and pay you back. But when you make a feast, ask the poor, the maimed, the lame, or the blind; and you will be blessed, because they don't have the resources to repay you. For you will be repaid in the resurrection of the righteous."*

When one of those who sat at the table with him heard these things, he said to him, *"Blessed is he who will feast in God's Kingdom!"*

But he said to him, *"A certain man made a great supper, and he invited many people. He sent out his servant at supper time to tell those who were invited, 'Come, for everything is ready now.' They all as one began to make excuses.*

"The first said to him, 'I have bought a field, and I must go and see it. Please have me excused.'

"Another said, 'I have bought five yoke of oxen, and I must go try them out. Please have me excused.'

"Another said, 'I have married a wife, and therefore I can't come.'

"That servant came, and told his lord these things. Then the master of the house, being angry, said to his servant, 'Go out quickly into the streets and lanes of the city, and bring in the poor, maimed, blind, and lame.'

"The servant said, 'Lord, it is done as you commanded, and there is still room.'

"The lord said to the servant, 'Go out into the highways and hedges, and compel them to come in, that my house may be filled. For I tell you that none of those men who were invited will taste of my supper.'"

Now great multitudes were going with him. He turned and said to them, *"If anyone comes to me, and doesn't disregard his own father, mother, wife, children, brothers, and sisters, yes, and his own life also, he can't be my disciple. Whoever doesn't bear his own cross, and come after me, can't be my disciple.*

"For which of you, desiring to build a tower, doesn't first sit down and count the cost, to see if he has enough to complete it? Or perhaps, when he has laid a foundation, and is not able to finish, everyone who sees begins to mock him, saying, 'This man began to build, and wasn't able to finish.' Or what king, as he goes to encounter another king in war, will not sit down first and consider whether he is able with ten thousand to meet him who comes against him with twenty thousand? Or else, while the other is yet a great way off, he sends an envoy, and asks for conditions of peace. So therefore whoever of you who doesn't renounce all that he has, he can't be my disciple. Salt is good, but if the salt becomes flat and tasteless, with what do you season it? It is fit neither for the soil nor for the manure pile. It is thrown out. He who has ears to hear, let him hear."

ARCHAEOLOGICAL AND HISTORICAL EVIDENCE:

Chapters 14 through 16 primarily consist of Jesus's teachings. Therefore, we won't have archaeological findings which relate directly to these three teaching chapters. Jesus's teachings in these chapters indicate Jesus was a preacher and a teacher, and the four Gospel books bound into the Bible are the primary evidence of Jesus's teachings.

WHAT DO YOU THINK?

➢ Where in today's society do you see people exalting themselves and putting themselves first? How would society change if the "Me First" attitude didn't exist anywhere in society?

➤ What is wrong with buttering people up and expecting something in return? Why do you think Jesus advocates serving people without regard to their background or their ability to return the favor?

___

➤ Who are the people invited into God's Kingdom, but who aren't willing to come? What makes people unwilling to come into God's Kingdom?

___

➤ Why do you think people make many excuses, with "I'll worry about it later" attitudes, toward God? Why don't they take the opportunity to walk with God seriously while they are alive on earth?

___

➤ Who are the people in the streets and lanes of the city, on the highways, and in the hedges of today's society? What do you think exists in their spirits which makes them willing to come to Jesus, when others put their personal needs and desires ahead of seeking God?

___

➤ What do you perceive is the cost of following Jesus in today's society?

➤ Jesus indicates you are either all in or all out of following Him. Why can't people half-heartedly follow Jesus and still be considered true followers of Jesus?

CHAPTER 15

Now all the tax collectors and sinners were coming close to him to hear him. The Pharisees and the scribes murmured, saying, "This man welcomes sinners, and eats with them."

He told them this parable. *"Which of you men, if you had one hundred sheep, and lost one of them, wouldn't leave the ninety-nine in the wilderness, and go after the one that was lost, until he found it? When he has found it, he carries it on his shoulders, rejoicing. When he comes home, he calls together his friends and his neighbors, saying to them, 'Rejoice with me, for I have found my sheep which was lost!' I tell you that even so there will be more joy in heaven over one sinner who repents, than over ninety-nine righteous people who need no repentance. Or what woman, if she had ten drachma coins, if she lost one drachma coin, wouldn't light a lamp, sweep the house, and seek diligently until she found it? When she has found it, she calls together her friends and neighbors, saying, 'Rejoice with me, for I have found the drachma which I had lost.' Even so, I tell you, there is joy in the presence of the angels of God over one sinner repenting."*

He said, "*A certain man had two sons. The younger of them said to his father, 'Father, give me my share of your property.' He divided his livelihood between them. Not many days after, the younger son gathered all of this together and traveled into a far country. There he wasted his property with riotous living. When he had spent all of it, there arose a severe famine in that country, and he began to be in need. He went and joined himself to one of the citizens of that country, and he sent him into his fields to feed pigs. He wanted to fill his belly with the husks that the pigs ate, but no one gave him any. But when he came to himself he said, 'How many hired servants of my father's have bread enough to spare, and I'm dying with hunger! I will get up and go to my father, and will tell him, "Father, I have sinned against heaven, and in your sight. I am no more worthy to be called your son. Make me as one of your hired servants."'*

"*He arose, and came to his father. But while he was still far off, his father saw him, and was moved with compassion, and ran, and fell on his neck, and kissed him. The son said to him, 'Father, I have sinned against heaven and in your sight. I am no longer worthy to be called your son.'*

"*But the father said to his servants, 'Bring out the best robe, and put it on him. Put a ring on his hand, and sandals on his feet. Bring the fattened calf, kill it, and let's eat, and celebrate; for this, my son, was dead, and is alive again. He was lost, and is found.' Then they began to celebrate.*

"*Now his elder son was in the field. As he came near to the house, he heard music and dancing. He called one of the servants to him, and asked what was going on. He said to him, 'Your brother has come, and your father has killed the fattened calf, because he has received him back safe and healthy.' But he was angry, and would not go in. Therefore his father came out, and begged him. But he answered his father, 'Behold, these many years I have served you, and I never disobeyed a commandment of yours, but you never gave me a goat, that I might celebrate with my friends. But when this your son came, who has devoured your living with prostitutes, you killed the fattened calf for him.'*

"He said to him, 'Son, you are always with me, and all that is mine is yours.

But it was appropriate to celebrate and be glad, for this, your brother, was dead, and is alive again. He was lost, and is found.'"

ARCHAEOLOGICAL AND HISTORICAL EVIDENCE:

Remember, chapters 14 through 16 are primarily chapters of Jesus's teachings, therefore we don't have historic or archaeological evidence to cover in this chapter. Again, the questions in this chapter will be reflective and life application questions for you to consider.

WHAT DO YOU THINK?

➢ If Jesus welcomes and eats with sinners, what kinds of things do you think Jesus expects us to do for sinners we know?

➢ Who is one lost person that you would save, if you could? What is something you can do to encourage and celebrate that person?

➢ What is worth so much to you that you are willing go out of your way to diligently seek it?

➤ No matter how much of a sinner anyone has been, God will welcome them with open arms when they come repenting and humbly seeking Him. How does God's loving, forgiving acceptance of all sinners encourage you in your relationship with God?

___

➤ It's human nature to compare our workload and compensation to other people's compensation. In the parable of the Prodigal Son, what is the Father's everlasting assurance to his son, when it comes to rewards for good work? Through this parable, what assurances does Jesus give us as children of God?

___

➤ What kind(s) of things have you done which you are sorry you did? If you believe God is real, consider taking time right now to apologize to God for any sins you've committed and ask for His forgiveness.

___

CHAPTER 16

He also said to his disciples, *"There was a certain rich man who had a manager. An accusation was made to him that this man was wasting his possessions. He called him, and said to him, 'What is this that I hear about you? Give an accounting of your management, for you can no longer be manager.'*

"The manager said within himself, 'What will I do, seeing that my lord is taking away the management position from me? I don't have strength to dig. I am ashamed to beg. I know what I will do, so that when I am removed from management, they may receive me into their houses.' Calling each one of his lord's debtors to him, he said to the first, 'How much do you owe to my lord?' He said, 'A hundred batos of oil.' He said to him, 'Take your bill, and sit down quickly and write fifty.' Then he said to another, 'How much do you owe?' He said, 'A hundred cors of wheat.' He said to him, 'Take your bill, and write eighty.'

"His lord commended the dishonest manager because he had done wisely, for the children of this world are, in their own generation, wiser than the children of the light. I tell you,

make for yourselves friends by means of unrighteous mammon, so that when you fail, they may receive you into the eternal tents. He who is faithful in a very little is faithful also in much. He who is dishonest in a very little is also dishonest in much. If therefore you have not been faithful in the unrighteous mammon, who will commit to your trust the true riches? If you have not been faithful in that which is another's, who will give you that which is your own? No servant can serve two masters, for either he will hate the one, and love the other; or else he will hold to one, and despise the other. You aren't able to serve God and Mammon."

The Pharisees, who were lovers of money, also heard all these things, and they scoffed at him. He said to them, *"You are those who justify yourselves in the sight of men, but God knows your hearts. For that which is exalted among men is an abomination in the sight of God. The law and the prophets were until John. From that time the Good News of God's Kingdom is preached, and everyone is forcing his way into it. But it is easier for heaven and earth to pass away, than for one tiny stroke of a pen in the law to fall. Everyone who divorces his wife and marries another commits adultery. He who marries one who is divorced from a husband commits adultery.*

"Now there was a certain rich man, and he was clothed in purple and fine linen, living in luxury every day. A certain beggar, named Lazarus, was taken to his gate, full of sores, and desiring to be fed with the crumbs that fell from the rich man's table. Yes, even the dogs came and licked his sores.

"The beggar died, and he was carried away by the angels to Abraham's bosom. The rich man also died, and was buried. In Hades, he lifted up his eyes, being in torment, and saw Abraham far off, and Lazarus at his bosom. He cried and said, 'Father Abraham, have mercy on me, and send Lazarus, that he may dip the tip of his finger in water, and cool my tongue! For I am in anguish in this flame.'

"But Abraham said, 'Son, remember that you, in your lifetime, received your good things, and Lazarus, in the same way, bad things. But here he is now comforted, and you are in anguish. Besides all this, between us and you there is a great gulf fixed, that those who want to pass from here to you are not able, and that no one may cross over from there to us.'

"He said, 'I ask you therefore, father, that you would send him to my father's house; for I have five brothers, that he may testify to them, so they won't also come into this place of torment.'

"But Abraham said to him, 'They have Moses and the prophets. Let them listen to them.'

"He said, 'No, father Abraham, but if one goes to them from the dead, they will repent.'

"He said to him, 'If they don't listen to Moses and the prophets, neither will they be persuaded if one rises from the dead.' "

ARCHAEOLOGICAL AND HISTORICAL EVIDENCE:

Chapter 16 is a chapter entirely composed of Jesus's teachings. Therefore the questions for this chapter will primarily be reflective and life application questions.

WHAT DO YOU THINK?

➢ When it comes to a person's soul, what difference do you think it makes whether his riches are earned wickedly or are earned in a righteous way?

➢ What kinds of things do people routinely do, which are encouraged behaviors, but would be considered an abomination in the sight of God?

- If everything on the planet Earth belongs to God, how do you think God expects us to handle the material possessions we have while we are living on this Earth?

  _____
  _____
  _____
  _____
  _____
  _____
  _____
  _____

- When it comes to handling money, Jesus says the children of this world (unbelievers) are shrewder than the children of the light (God's people). In what ways do you see this is true? What do you think God's people need to do to become wiser when handling money?

  _____
  _____
  _____
  _____
  _____
  _____
  _____
  _____

- If the way we handle our money and possessions in life dictates what God will give us in heaven, what are some wise ways for people handle or use their money on earth, if they want God to give them true riches in heaven?

  _____
  _____
  _____
  _____
  _____
  _____
  _____
  _____

➢ Jesus talks about the rich man in Hades (hell), and the poor beggar, Lazarus, in heaven. What do you believe is the main point in this story about the rich man and the beggar?

➢ What makes it difficult for people to accept the existence of hell? What makes most people think they are destined for heaven, along with most everyone they know, regardless of what they do?

➢ At the end of chapter 16, Jesus says if people won't listen to Moses and the prophets, neither will they be persuaded if one rises from the dead. Jesus rose from the dead, and many people in His day believed in Him, but others did not. What do you suppose was the difference between those who believed in Jesus and His resurrection and those who did not? What do you think makes the difference today in whether people believe in Jesus and His resurrection or not?

CHAPTER 17

He said to the disciples, *"It is impossible that no occasions of stumbling should come, but woe to him through whom they come! It would be better for him if a millstone were hung around his neck, and he were thrown into the sea, rather than that he should cause one of these little ones to stumble. Be careful. If your brother sins against you, rebuke him. If he repents, forgive him. If he sins against you seven times in the day, and seven times returns, saying, 'I repent,' you shall forgive him."*

The apostles said to the Lord, "Increase our faith."

The Lord said, *"If you had faith like a grain of mustard seed, you would tell this sycamore tree, 'Be uprooted, and be planted in the sea,' and it would obey you. But who is there among you, having a servant plowing or keeping sheep, that will say when he comes in from the field, 'Come immediately and sit down at the table,' and will not rather tell him, 'Prepare my supper, clothe yourself properly, and serve me, while I eat and drink. Afterward you shall eat and drink'? Does he thank that servant because he did the things that were commanded? I think not. Even so you also, when you have done all the things that are commanded you, say, 'We are unworthy servants. We have done our duty.'"*

As he was on his way to Jerusalem, he was passing along the borders of Samaria and Galilee. As he entered into a certain village, ten men who were lepers met him, who stood at a distance. They lifted up their voices, saying, "Jesus, Master, have mercy on us!"

When he saw them, he said to them, *"Go and show yourselves to the priests."* As they went, they were cleansed. One of them, when he saw that he was healed, turned back, glorifying God with a loud voice. He fell on his face at Jesus' feet, giving him thanks; and he was a Samaritan. Jesus answered, *"Weren't the ten cleansed? But where are the nine? Were there none found who returned to give glory to God, except this foreigner?"*

Then he said to him, *"Get up, and go your way. Your faith has healed you."*

Being asked by the Pharisees when God's Kingdom would come, he answered them, *"God's Kingdom doesn't come with observation; neither will they say, 'Look, here!' or, 'Look, there!' for behold, God's Kingdom is within you."*

He said to the disciples, *"The days will come when you will desire to see one of the days of the Son of Man, and you will not see it. They will tell you, 'Look, here!' or 'Look, there!' Don't go away or follow after them, for as the lightning, when it flashes out of one part under the sky, shines to another part under the sky; so will the Son of Man be in his day. But first, he must suffer many things and be rejected by this generation. As it was in the days of Noah, even so will it be also in the days of the Son of Man. They ate, they drank, they married, and they were given in marriage until the day that Noah entered into the ship, and the flood came and destroyed them all.*

"Likewise, even as it was in the days of Lot: they ate, they drank, they bought, they sold, they planted, they built; but in the day that Lot went out from Sodom, it rained fire and sulfur from the sky and destroyed them all.

"It will be the same way in the day that the Son of Man is revealed. In that day, he who will be on the housetop and his goods in the house, let him not go down to take them away. Let him who is in the field likewise not turn back. Remember Lot's wife! Whoever seeks to save his life loses it, but whoever loses his life preserves it. I tell you, in that night there will be two people in one bed. One will be taken and the other will be left. There will be two grinding grain together. One will be taken and the other will be left."

They, answering, asked him, "Where, Lord?"

He said to them, *"Where the body is, there the vultures will also be gathered together."*

ARCHAEOLOGICAL AND HISTORICAL EVIDENCE:

Samaria is the only new place or person mentioned in this chapter. Samaria was a thriving City that differed greatly from Jerusalem in the era of Jesus. Samaria is a city that was "ruled by coercion." The region of Galilee and Samaria are adjacent to each other, so it is factual that a person can pass along the border between these two existing geographic locations, just as Luke 17 says that Jesus did (17.1).

WHAT DO YOU THINK?

➢ Jesus says, *"It is impossible that no occasions for stumbling should come, but woe to him through whom they come!"* Given this teaching of Jesus', what do you think will be the punishment for those who cause people to turn away from or against God and/or Jesus?

➢ Jesus tells us to forgive people every time they ask for forgiveness. What makes this a difficult way to deal with people who do things which harm you? What kinds of thoughts about the person can you focus on, which might make it easier for you to genuinely forgive them?

_____
_____
_____
_____
_____
_____
_____
_____

➢ As a servant who's just doing his duty, we are not to expect anything in return for doing what is right. What are some things people commonly hope for or expect from others when helping them?

_____
_____
_____
_____
_____
_____
_____
_____

➢ There was only one of the 10 healed lepers who returned to thank Jesus. How does this reflect on the hearts and attitudes of the other nine lepers? What similarities do you see between them and people in today's society?

_____
_____
_____
_____
_____
_____
_____
_____

➤ Jesus says God's kingdom is within us. From this, what is your understanding of the spiritual world and how it relates to your soul?

___

➤ Jesus says when he returns to earth, He will come like lightning in the sky and people will be taken up to be with Him. If a person doesn't believe in Jesus on that day, why is it important for them to already know and understand what Jesus taught and prophesied?

___

CHAPTER 18

He also spoke a parable to them that they must always pray, and not give up, saying, *"There was a judge in a certain city who didn't fear God, and didn't respect man. A widow was in that city, and she often came to him, saying, 'Defend me from my adversary!' He wouldn't for a while, but afterward he said to himself, 'Though I neither fear God, nor respect man, yet because this widow bothers me, I will defend her, or else she will wear me out by her continual coming.'"*

The Lord said, *"Listen to what the unrighteous judge says. Won't God avenge his chosen ones who are crying out to him day and night, and yet he exercises patience with them? I tell you that he will avenge them quickly. Nevertheless, when the Son of Man comes, will he find faith on the earth?"*

He spoke also this parable to certain people who were convinced of their own righteousness, and who despised all others. *"Two men went up into the temple to pray; one was a Pharisee, and the other was a tax collector. The Pharisee stood and prayed to himself like this:*

'God, I thank you that I am not like the rest of men, extortionists, unrighteous, adulterers, or even like this tax collector. I fast twice a week. I give tithes of all that I get.' But the tax collector, standing far away, wouldn't even lift up his eyes to heaven, but beat his breast, saying, 'God, be merciful to me, a sinner!' I tell you, this man went down to his house justified rather than the other; for everyone who exalts himself will be humbled, but he who humbles himself will be exalted."

They were also bringing their babies to him, that he might touch them. But when the disciples saw it, they rebuked them. Jesus summoned them, saying, *"Allow the little children to come to me, and don't hinder them, for God's Kingdom belongs to such as these. Most certainly, I tell you, whoever doesn't receive God's Kingdom like a little child, he will in no way enter into it."*

A certain ruler asked him, saying, "Good Teacher, what shall I do to inherit eternal life?"

Jesus asked him, *"Why do you call me good? No one is good, except one: God. You know the commandments: 'Don't commit adultery,' 'Don't murder,' 'Don't steal,' 'Don't give false testimony,' 'Honor your father and your mother.'"*

He said, "I have observed all these things from my youth up."

When Jesus heard these things, he said to him, *"You still lack one thing. Sell all that you have, and distribute it to the poor. Then you will have treasure in heaven; then come, follow me."*

But when he heard these things, he became very sad, for he was very rich.

Jesus, seeing that he became very sad, said, *"How hard it is for those who have riches to enter into God's Kingdom! For it is easier for a camel to enter in through a needle's eye than for a rich man to enter into God's Kingdom."*

Those who heard it said, "Then who can be saved?"

But he said, *"The things which are impossible with men are possible with God."*

Peter said, "Look, we have left everything and followed you."

He said to them, *"Most certainly I tell you, there is no one who has left house, or wife, or brothers, or parents, or children, for God's Kingdom's sake, who will not receive many times more in this time, and in the world to come, eternal life."*

He took the twelve aside, and said to them, *"Behold, we are going up to Jerusalem, and all the things that are written through the prophets concerning the Son of Man will be completed. For he will be delivered up to the Gentiles, will be mocked, treated shamefully, and spit on. They will scourge and kill him. On the third day, he will rise again."*

They understood none of these things. This saying was hidden from them, and they didn't understand the things that were said. As he came near Jericho, a certain blind man sat by the road, begging. Hearing a multitude going by, he asked what this meant. They told him that Jesus of Nazareth was passing by. He cried out, "Jesus, you son of David, have mercy on me!" Those who led the way rebuked him, that he should be quiet; but he cried out all the more, "You son of David, have mercy on me!"

Standing still, Jesus commanded him to be brought to him. When he had come near, he asked him, *"What do you want me to do?"*

He said, "Lord, that I may see again."

Jesus said to him, *"Receive your sight. Your faith has healed you."*

Immediately he received his sight and followed him, glorifying God. All the people, when they saw it, praised God.

ARCHAEOLOGICAL AND HISTORICAL EVIDENCE:

Jericho is mentioned frequently in the Bible. "Excavations have revealed that Jericho is one of the earliest settlements dating back to 9000 B.C. It also has the oldest known protective wall in the world" (18.1). "Jericho is known as the oldest continuously inhabited city in the world. Jericho also claims the record for the lowest city in the world at over 800 feet (250 meters) below sea level" (18.2).

Other than the mention of the city of Jericho, most of chapter 18 is another chapter full of Jesus's teachings, rather than action. Therefore, once again you will find reflection and life application types of questions below.

WHAT DO YOU THINK?

➢ Jesus tells us we must always pray, and not give up. What affect do you think there is on people's lives when they don't pray at all? What positive affect(s) do you think prayer can provide?

_____
_____
_____
_____
_____
_____
_____

➢ To whom do you relate more: the righteous Pharisee, or the distraught tax collector? In what ways might you be similar to each of them?

_____
_____
_____
_____
_____
_____
_____

➢ What does it look like to receive God's kingdom like a little child?

_____
_____
_____
_____
_____
_____
_____

➢ What does selling everything and giving it to the poor demonstrate about someone's heart and soul?

_____
_____
_____
_____
_____
_____
_____
_____

➢ What kinds of things seem impossible for you to achieve in your life? Would these things be possible for God to accomplish? Why would or wouldn't God be willing to help everyone achieve everything they ever desired?

_____
_____
_____
_____
_____
_____
_____
_____

➢ Jesus told his disciples (again) what would happen to Him in the city of Jerusalem before it happened. What does Jesus's prophecy demonstrate about His knowledge of the future?

_____
_____
_____
_____
_____
_____
_____
_____

CHAPTER 19

He entered and was passing through Jericho. There was a man named Zacchaeus. He was a chief tax collector, and he was rich. He was trying to see who Jesus was, and couldn't because of the crowd, because he was short. He ran on ahead, and climbed up into a sycamore tree to see him, for he was going to pass that way. When Jesus came to the place, he looked up and saw him, and said to him, *"Zacchaeus, hurry and come down, for today I must stay at your house."* He hurried, came down, and received him joyfully. When they saw it, they all murmured, saying, "He has gone in to lodge with a man who is a sinner."

Zacchaeus stood and said to the Lord, "Behold, Lord, half of my goods I give to the poor. If I have wrongfully exacted anything of anyone, I restore four times as much."

Jesus said to him, *"Today, salvation has come to this house, because he also is a son of Abraham. For the Son of Man came to seek and to save that which was lost."*

As they heard these things, he went on and told a parable, because he was near Jerusalem, and they supposed that God's Kingdom would be revealed immediately. He said therefore, *"A certain nobleman went into a far country to receive for himself a kingdom and to return. He called ten servants of his and gave them ten mina coins, and told them, 'Conduct business until I come.' But his citizens hated him, and sent an envoy after him, saying, 'We don't want this man to reign over us.'*

"When he had come back again, having received the kingdom, he commanded these servants, to whom he had given the money, to be called to him, that he might know what they had gained by conducting business. The first came before him, saying, 'Lord, your mina has made ten more minas.'

"He said to him, 'Well done, you good servant! Because you were found faithful with very little, you shall have authority over ten cities.'

"The second came, saying, 'Your mina, Lord, has made five minas.'

"So he said to him, 'And you are to be over five cities.'

Another came, saying, 'Lord, behold, your mina, which I kept laid away in a handkerchief, for I feared you, because you are an exacting man. You take up that which you didn't lay down, and reap that which you didn't sow.' *"He said to him, 'Out of your own mouth I will judge you, you wicked servant! You knew that I am an exacting man, taking up that which I didn't lay down, and reaping that which I didn't sow. Then why didn't you deposit my money in the bank, and at my coming, I might have earned interest on it?' He said to those who stood by, 'Take the mina away from him and give it to him who has the ten minas.'*

"They said to him, 'Lord, he has ten minas!' *'For I tell you that to everyone who has, will more be given; but from him who doesn't have, even that which he has will be taken away from him. But bring those enemies of mine who didn't want me to reign over them here, and kill them before me.' "*

Having said these things, he went on ahead, going up to Jerusalem.

When he came near to Bethsphage and Bethany, at the mountain that is called Olivet, he sent two of his disciples, saying, *"Go your way into the village on the other side, in which, as you enter, you will find a colt tied, which no man had ever sat upon. Untie it and bring it. If anyone asks you, 'Why are you untying it?' say to him: 'The Lord needs it.'"*

Those who were sent went away, and found things just as he had told them. As they were untying the colt, its owners said to them, "Why are you untying the colt?"

They said, "The Lord needs it." Then they brought it to Jesus. They threw their cloaks on the colt, and sat Jesus on them. As he went, they spread their cloaks on the road. As he was now getting near, at the descent of the Mount of Olives, the whole multitude of the disciples began to rejoice and praise God with a loud voice for all the mighty works which they had seen, saying, "Blessed is the King who comes in the name of the Lord! Peace in heaven, and glory in the highest!"

Some of the Pharisees from the multitude said to him, "Teacher, rebuke your disciples!"

He answered them, *"I tell you that if these were silent, the stones would cry out."*

When he came near, he saw the city and wept over it, saying, *"If you, even you, had known today the things which belong to your peace! But now, they are hidden from your eyes. For the days will come on you, when your enemies will throw up a barricade against you, surround you, hem you in on every side, and will dash you and your children within you to the ground. They will not leave in you one stone on another, because you didn't know the time of your visitation."*

He entered into the temple, and began to drive out those who bought and sold in it, saying to them, *"It is written, 'My house is a house of prayer,' but you have made it a 'den of robbers'!"*

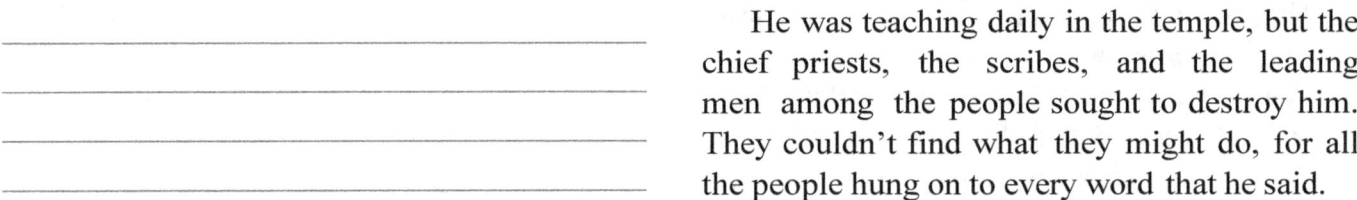

He was teaching daily in the temple, but the chief priests, the scribes, and the leading men among the people sought to destroy him. They couldn't find what they might do, for all the people hung on to every word that he said.

ARCHAEOLOGICAL AND HISTORICAL EVIDENCE:

In this chapter, Jesus moves through several towns. Therefore, we have historical and archaeological information to reference.

First, "Zacchaeus' Sycamore Tree is one of the top tourist attractions in Jericho due to the role it played in a famous New Testament event (in this chapter). The tree stands at a major intersection in Jericho. The tree may or may not be the one Zacchaeus actually climbed, but local tradition has named it Zacchaeus' Tree. Tests carried out on the tree have shown it is over 2,000 years old and it stands in the same setting as the Biblical sycamore tree" (19.0).

We know from ancient history, in the days of Jesus, Romans collected taxes from every person in every town in their jurisdiction. "The Romans hired local men to collect the taxes for them. The local tax collectors made their living off how much extra money they were able to charge people—over and above the legal taxes" (19.1). According to the Bible, Zacchaeus was a typical tax collector of the day. He charged more than what was owed, so he could pad his own pockets and make a good living.

"Bethany is located at the site now also known by the Arabic name al-Eizariya" (19.2). It was the home of Mary, Martha, and Lazarus in the Bible. "The oldest house in present-day al-Eizariya, is a 2,000+ year-old dwelling reputed to have been the house of Martha and Mary" (19.2). There is also a cave which is said to be the tomb of Lazarus there.

"Archaeological finds in the vicinity of Bethphage include caves, coins, cisterns, pools, a wine press, and various types of tombs" (19.3). "About a 2 kilometer or less walk from the eastern walls of Jerusalem, Bethphage was on the way to Jerusalem from Bethany. The modern village of Al Tur probably is situated over the ancient site, although the nearby village of Abu Dis, farther to the south and closer to Bethany, has also been suggested. Today, the Church of Bethphage stands within the boundaries of what is thought to be ancient Bethphage" (19.4).

The Mount of Olives or Mount Olivet is "a mountain ridge east of and adjacent to Jerusalem's Old City. It is named for the olive groves that once covered its slopes" (19.5). "The mount has been used as a Jewish cemetery for over 3,000 years and holds approximately 150,000 graves, making it central in the tradition of Jewish cemeteries. Several key events in the life of Jesus, as related in the Gospels, took place on the Mount of Olives, and in the Acts of the Apostles, it is described as the place from which Jesus ascended to heaven. Because of its association with both Jesus and Mary, the mount has been a site of Christian worship since ancient times" (19.5).

Here we have additional archaeologic sites, reputed as being related to key Biblical people, which have been held in high regard for centuries. As people living centuries later, we must consider the likelihood the ancient people were knowledgeable about their communities and sincere in their reverence of the places related to the life of Jesus. Are there legitimate reasons for people today to doubt the preserved knowledge of people living in the first century A.D.?

WHAT DO YOU THINK?

➤ If Zacchaeus was a short man, there are sycamore trees in Jericho, and Jesus was famous, what makes the story about Zacchaeus climbing a tree to see Jesus believable? Explain your thoughts.

➤ Why were the religious leaders so upset that Jesus went to stay at Zacchaeus' house? If they didn't like Jesus, why would they care if Jesus went to Zacchaeus' house?

➤ Jericho, the Mount of Olives, Bethany, and Bethphage are Biblical hot spots on earth. If you travel to the Middle East, which of these areas would you be most interested in seeing? What fascinates you most about that area of the world?

➤ Some Biblical tourist destinations today may be partially based on local folklore, rather than being grounded in provable, concrete evidence. In what ways can folklore have a factual basis, and how can we figure out what aspects are likely to be true versus fictional?

___

➤ In this chapter, Jesus prophecies His disciples will find a colt in town. According to Luke's research, that's exactly what happened. How do you think this prophecy fulfillment would affect your belief in Jesus, if you were one of the disciples who went to get the colt and everything happened exactly as Jesus said it would?

___

➤ Jesus predicted the Temple in Jerusalem would be destroyed, hemmed in on every side and dashed by its enemies. The Book of Luke was written before the temple in Jerusalem was destroyed in 70 A.D. The Temple is archaeologically verified as a building which stood and was destroyed. In what way do Jesus's prophecies, Luke's writing the prediction about the temple before it was destroyed, and the destruction of the Temple, affect your belief about Jesus's ability to foresee future events?

___

CHAPTER 20

On one of those days, as he was teaching the people in the temple and preaching the Good News, the priests and scribes came to him with the elders. They asked him, "Tell us: by what authority do you do these things? Or who is giving you this authority?"

He answered them, *"I also will ask you one question. Tell me: the baptism of John, was it from heaven, or from men?"*

They reasoned with themselves, saying, "If we say, 'From heaven,' he will say, 'Why didn't you believe him?' But if we say, 'From men,' all the people will stone us, for they are persuaded that John was a prophet." They answered that they didn't know where it was from.

Jesus said to them, *"Neither will I tell you by what authority I do these things."*

He began to tell the people this parable. *"A man planted a vineyard, and rented it out to some farmers, and went into another country for a long time. At the proper season, he sent a servant to the farmers to collect his share of the fruit of the vineyard. But the farmers beat him, and sent him away empty.*

"He sent yet another servant, and they also beat him, and treated him shamefully, and sent him away empty. He sent yet a third, and they also wounded him, and threw him out. The lord of the vineyard said, 'What shall I do? I will send my beloved son. It may be that seeing him, they will respect him.'

"But when the farmers saw him, they reasoned among themselves, saying, 'This is the heir. Come, let's kill him, that the inheritance may be ours.' They threw him out of the vineyard and killed him. What therefore will the lord of the vineyard do to them? He will come and destroy these farmers, and will give the vineyard to others."

When they heard that, they said, "May that never be!"

But he looked at them and said, "Then what is this that is written,

'The stone which the builders rejected was made the chief cornerstone?'

"Everyone who falls on that stone will be broken to pieces, but it will crush whomever it falls on to dust."

The chief priests and the scribes sought to lay hands on him that very hour, but they feared the people — for they knew he had spoken this parable against them. They watched him and sent out spies, who pretended to be righteous, that they might trap him in something he said, so as to deliver him up to the power and authority of the governor. They asked him, "Teacher, we know that you say and teach what is right, and aren't partial to anyone, but truly teach the way of God. Is it lawful for us to pay taxes to Caesar, or not?"

But he perceived their craftiness, and said to them, "Why do you test me? Show me a denarius. Whose image and inscription are on it?"

They answered, "Caesar's."

He said to them, "Then give to Caesar the things that are Caesar's, and to God the things that are God's."

They weren't able to trap him in his words before the people. They marveled at his answer and were silent. Some of the Sadducees came to him, those who deny that there is a resurrection. They asked him, "Teacher, Moses wrote to us that if a man's brother dies having a wife, and he is childless, his brother should take the wife and raise up children for his brother. There were therefore seven brothers. The first took a wife, and died childless. The second took her as wife, and he died childless. The third took her, and likewise the seven all left no children, and died. Afterward the woman also died. Therefore in the resurrection whose wife of them will she be? For the seven had her as a wife."

Jesus said to them, *"The children of this age marry, and are given in marriage. But those who are considered worthy to attain to that age and the resurrection from the dead neither marry nor are given in marriage. For they can't die any more, for they are like the angels, and are children of God, being children of the resurrection. But that the dead are raised, even Moses showed at the bush, when he called the Lord 'The God of Abraham, the God of Isaac, and the God of Jacob.' Now he is not the God of the dead, but of the living, for all are alive to him."*

Some of the scribes answered, "Teacher, you speak well." They didn't dare to ask him any more questions.

He said to them, *"Why do they say that the Christ is David's son? David himself says in the book of Psalms,*

'The Lord said to my Lord, "Sit at my right hand, until I make your enemies the footstool of your feet."'

"David therefore calls him Lord, so how is he his son?"

In the hearing of all the people, he said to his disciples, *"Beware of those scribes who like to walk in long robes, and love greetings in the marketplaces, the best seats in the synagogues, and the best places at feasts; who devour widows' houses, and for a pretense make long prayers: these will receive greater condemnation."*

ARCHAEOLOGICAL AND HISTORICAL EVIDENCE:

The Smithsonian Magazine says, "The discoveries solidified the portrait of Jesus as a Jew preaching to other Jews" (20.1). The main question they had been trying to answer was whether there were synagogues for Jesus to preach to other Jews, and the answer is, YES!

"They found a synagogue from the time of Jesus, in the hometown of Mary Magdalene. Though big enough for just 200 people, it was, for its time and place, opulent. It had a mosaic floor; frescoes in pleasing geometries of red, yellow and blue; separate chambers for public Torah readings, private study and storage of the scrolls; a bowl outside for the ritual washing of hands" (20.1).

"In the center of the sanctuary, the archaeologists unearthed a mysterious stone block, the size of a toy chest, unlike anything anyone had seen before. Carved onto its faces were a seven-branched menorah, a chariot of fire and a hoard of symbols associated with the most hallowed precincts of the Jerusalem temple. The stone is already seen as one of the most important discoveries in biblical archaeology in decades" (20.1). Thus, we know beautiful synagogues existed in Jesus's day, in which He could preach and teach the Jewish people.

When it comes to the mention of Roman coins in this chapter, "Roman coins were first produced in the late 4th century B.C. in Italy and continued to be minted for another eight centuries across the empire. Denominations and values more or less constantly changed but certain types such as the sestertii and denarii would persist and come to rank amongst the most famous coins in history" (20.2).

"In c.211 B.C. a whole new coinage system was introduced. Appearing for the first time was the silver denarius (pl. denarii), a coin that would be the principal silver coin of Rome until the 3rd century CE. The denarius was equal to 10 bronze asses (sing. as), each of which weighed 54 g. or 2 oz." (20.2).

Numerous Roman coins have been found from the era of Jesus. You can easily do a search online to see images of the various coins that bore images of the Caesars.

"The Sadducees first appear in the historical record not as priests but as a political group. The Jewish historian Josephus mentions them in the context of John Hyrcanus, the Hasmonean high priest and ruler of Judah from 135-104 B.C. [..] Josephus tantalizingly mentions that the Sadducees ascribe authority to Scripture, not to the ancestral traditions handed down by the Pharisees" (20.3). From these independent historical documents, we know the Sadducees were an influential group of people who actually lived in the era of Jesus.

When it comes to this chapter's mention of Abraham, Isaac, Jacob, and David, it might be beneficial to refer back to the genealogy of Jesus in chapter 3. I won't spend time on additional archaeological or historic information about these men, since we covered them in earlier chapters, but I would encourage you to visit the https://www.biblicalarchaeology.org/ website, and search for the names of each of these individuals, if you are interested in learning more about them.

WHAT DO YOU THINK?

➢ Like speakers in various venues today, Jesus spoke in temples and synagogues wherever He traveled. The priests and scribes wanted to know where Jesus got His authority. In this instance, why do you think Jesus was evasive with His answer about from where His authority comes?

_____
_____
_____
_____
_____
_____
_____
_____

➢ The priests and scribes acknowledged Jesus taught the ways of God, but they didn't embrace Jesus's teachings or follow Him. What do you think the consequences were, and will be, for those who believe Jesus teaches the truth, but then refuse to follow Jesus and do what He says?

_____
_____
_____
_____
_____
_____
_____
_____

➢ The Sadducees were just one group of leaders in Jesus's day who held clout and wielded their authority in society. When it comes to groups of people in society today, which groups do you think would condemn or seek to murder Jesus if he lived on Earth today? Why do you think they would?

_____
_____
_____
_____
_____
_____
_____
_____

➢ Jesus said we become spiritual, like Angels, when we die. What aspects of yourself do you think will be part of your spiritual being when you transform from your physical body to a spiritual being?

___

➢ When Jesus taught the parable of the man who planted the vineyard, Jesus was talking about God as the man who planted. The farmers to which the vineyard was rented are the people God sent His prophets to warn and save them. And Jesus is the son sent by His Father. What do you think motivates people hate or kill people who are trying to bring them a message from God?

___

➢ Jesus says He is the cornerstone which the church leaders rejected, and He is the stone by which people fall or are broken. In what ways do people reject Jesus, and what consequences do you think they will suffer by failing to learn from and follow Jesus?

___

CHAPTER 21

He looked up and saw the rich people who were putting their gifts into the treasury. He saw a certain poor widow casting in two small brass coins. He said, *"Truly I tell you, this poor widow put in more than all of them, for all these put in gifts for God from their abundance, but she, out of her poverty, put in all that she had to live on."*

As some were talking about the temple and how it was decorated with beautiful stones and gifts, he said, *"As for these things which you see, the days will come, in which there will not be left here one stone on another that will not be thrown down."*

They asked him, "Teacher, so when will these things be? What is the sign that these things are about to happen?"

He said, *"Watch out that you don't get led astray, for many will come in my name, saying, 'I am he,' and, 'The time is at hand.' Therefore don't follow them. When you hear of wars and disturbances, don't be terrified, for these things must happen first, but the end won't come immediately."*

Then he said to them, *"Nation will rise against nation, and kingdom against kingdom. There will be great earthquakes, famines, and plagues in various places. There will be terrors and great signs from heaven. But before all these things, they will lay their hands on you and will persecute you, delivering you up to synagogues and prisons, bringing you before kings and governors for my name's sake. It will turn out as a testimony for you. Settle it therefore in your hearts not to meditate beforehand how to answer, for I will give you a mouth and wisdom which all your adversaries will not be able to withstand or to contradict. You will be handed over even by parents, brothers, relatives, and friends. They will cause some of you to be put to death. You will be hated by all men for my name's sake. And not a hair of your head will perish.*

"By your endurance you will win your lives.

"But when you see Jerusalem surrounded by armies, then know that its desolation is at hand. Then let those who are in Judea flee to the mountains. Let those who are in the middle of her depart. Let those who are in the country not enter therein. For these are days of vengeance, that all things which are written may be fulfilled. Woe to those who are pregnant and to those who nurse infants in those days! For there will be great distress in the land, and wrath to this people. They will fall by the edge of the sword, and will be led captive into all the nations. Jerusalem will be trampled down by the Gentiles, until the times of the Gentiles are fulfilled.

"There will be signs in the sun, moon, and stars; and on the earth anxiety of nations, in perplexity for the roaring of the sea and the waves; men fainting for fear, and for expectation of the things which are coming on the world: for the powers of the heavens will be shaken. Then they will see the Son of Man coming in a cloud with power and great glory. But when these things begin to happen,

look up and lift up your heads, because your redemption is near."

He told them a parable. *"See the fig tree and all the trees. When they are already budding, you see it and know by your own selves that the summer is already near. Even so you also, when you see these things happening, know that God's Kingdom is near. Most certainly I tell you, this generation will not pass away until all things are accomplished. Heaven and earth will pass away, but my words will by no means pass away.*

"So be careful, or your hearts will be loaded down with carousing, drunkenness, and cares of this life, and that day will come on you suddenly. For it will come like a snare on all those who dwell on the surface of all the earth. Therefore be watchful all the time, praying that you may be counted worthy to escape all these things that will happen, and to stand before the Son of Man."

Every day Jesus was teaching in the temple, and every night he would go out and spend the night on the mountain that is called Olivet. All the people came early in the morning to him in the temple to hear him.

ARCHAEOLOGICAL AND HISTORICAL EVIDENCE:

When Luke mentions the widow putting two small brass coins into the treasury, we can ask ourselves whether there really were Roman coins made of brass. "Augustus reformed the denominations of smaller coins and his new system would form the basis of Roman coinage for the next three centuries. Gone were the silver coins below the denarius to be replaced in 23 B.C. by the brass (copper and zinc) orichalcum sestertius and dupondius (pl. dupondii), and the *as* and the even smaller quadran (quarter) were now made from copper instead of bronze" (21.1). We have confirmation there were small brass coins in our historical documentation and in the artifacts.

In this chapter, we also see people were talking about how the temple was decorated with beautiful stones and gifts. In the previous chapter, we read about an archaeological dig located in the hometown of Mary Magdalene, which is the location of an opulent synagogue. From the dig in Mary's hometown and the mention of the beautiful synagogue in this chapter, we can conclude Luke's reference is likely to be accurate when he mentions a beautiful synagogue in which Jesus was teaching.

WHAT DO YOU THINK?

➤ In this chapter, Jesus prophesied nation would rise against nation, kingdom against kingdom, there will be great earthquakes, famines and plagues in various places. When you look at the world today, what are your thoughts about the accuracy of this prophecy made by Jesus 2,000+ years ago?

_____
_____
_____
_____
_____
_____
_____
_____

➤ Jesus tells us not to be led astray, and not to be worried or terrified about things to come, because they are necessary. How can you prepare your mind and heart for the things Jesus tells us will occur?

_____
_____
_____
_____
_____
_____
_____
_____

➤ In this chapter, Jesus also says there will be "on the earth anxiety of nations, in perplexity for the roaring of the sea and the waves, men fainting for fear, and for expectation of the things which are coming on the world." What relationship do you see between Jesus's prophecy and people's concerns over global warming, climate change, and about the political climate around the world today?

_____
_____
_____
_____
_____
_____
_____
_____

- Jesus says, His Words will not pass away, and they haven't yet. What do you think makes Jesus's words timeless and everlasting?

- Jesus says, "Watch out that you don't get led astray, for many will come in my name, saying, 'I am he,' and, 'The time is at hand.' Therefore don't follow them. When you hear of wars and disturbances, don't be terrified, for these things must happen first, but the end won't come immediately." Does Jesus's reassurance help you stay free of fear when there are wars, disturbances, great earthquakes, famines, and plagues? How does it help, or why doesn't it help?

- Jesus says there will be signs, and THEN people will see the Son of Man (Jesus) coming in a cloud with power and great glory. Which of the signs Jesus mentioned do you see in the world today?

CHAPTER 22

Now the feast of unleavened bread, which is called the Passover, was approaching. The chief priests and the scribes sought how they might put him to death, for they feared the people. Satan entered into Judas, who was also called Iscariot, who was counted with the twelve. He went away, and talked with the chief priests and captains about how he might deliver him to them. They were glad, and agreed to give him money. He consented, and sought an opportunity to deliver him to them in the absence of the multitude. The day of unleavened bread came, on which the Passover must be sacrificed. Jesus sent Peter and John, saying, *"Go and prepare the Passover for us, that we may eat."*

They said to him, "Where do you want us to prepare?"

He said to them, *"Behold, when you have entered into the city, a man carrying a pitcher of water will meet you. Follow him into the house which he enters. Tell the master of the house, 'The Teacher says to you, "Where is the guest room, where I may eat the Passover with my disciples?"' He will show you a large, furnished upper room. Make preparations there."*

They went, found things as Jesus had told them, and they prepared the Passover. When the hour had come, he sat down with the twelve apostles. He said to them, *"I have earnestly desired to eat this Passover with you before I suffer, for I tell you, I will no longer by any means eat of it until it is fulfilled in God's Kingdom."*

He received a cup, and when he had given thanks, he said, *"Take this, and share it among yourselves, for I tell you, I will not drink at all again from the fruit of the vine, until God's Kingdom comes."*

He took bread, and when he had given thanks, he broke, and gave it to them, saying, *"This is my body which is given for you. Do this in memory of me."*

Likewise, he took the cup after supper, saying, *"This cup is the new covenant in my blood, which is poured out for you. But behold, the hand of him who betrays me is with me on the table. The Son of Man indeed goes, as it has been determined, but woe to that man through whom he is betrayed!"*

They began to question among themselves, which of them it was who would do this thing. A dispute also arose among them, which of them was considered to be greatest.

He said to them, *"The kings of the nations lord it over them, and those who have authority over them are called 'benefactors.' But not so with you. But one who is the greater among you, let him become as the younger, and one who is governing, as one who serves. For who is greater, one who sits at the table, or one who serves? Isn't it he who sits at the table? But I am among you as one who serves. But you are those who have continued with me in my trials. I confer on you a kingdom, even as my Father conferred on me, that you may eat and drink at my table in my Kingdom. You will sit on thrones, judging the twelve tribes of Israel."*

The Lord said, *"Simon, Simon, behold, Satan asked to have all of you, that he might sift you as wheat, but I prayed for you, that your faith wouldn't fail. You, when once you have turned again, establish your brothers."*

He said to him, "Lord, I am ready to go with you both to prison and to death!"

He said, *"I tell you, Peter, the rooster will by no means crow today until you deny that you know me three times."*

He said to them, *"When I sent you out without purse, wallet, and sandals, did you lack anything?"*

They said, "Nothing."

Then he said to them, *"But now, whoever has a purse, let him take it, and likewise a wallet. Whoever has none, let him sell his cloak, and buy a sword. For I tell you that this which is written must still be fulfilled in me: 'He was counted with transgressors.' For that which concerns me has an end."*

They said, "Lord, behold, here are two swords."

He said to them, *"That is enough."*

He came out and went, as his custom was, to the Mount of Olives. His disciples also followed him. When he was at the place, he said to them, *"Pray that you don't enter into temptation."*

He was withdrawn from them about a stone's throw, and he knelt down and prayed, saying, *"Father, if you are willing, remove this cup from me. Nevertheless, not my will, but yours, be done."*

An angel from heaven appeared to him, strengthening him. Being in agony he prayed more earnestly. His sweat became like great drops of blood falling down on the ground.

When he rose up from his prayer, he came to the disciples, and found them sleeping because of grief, and said to them, *"Why do you sleep? Rise and pray that you may not enter into temptation."*

While he was still speaking, behold, a multitude, and he who was called Judas, one of the twelve, was leading them. He came near to Jesus to kiss him. But Jesus said to him, *"Judas, do you betray the Son of Man with a kiss?"*

When those who were around him saw what was about to happen, they said to him, "Lord, shall we strike with the sword?" A certain one of them struck the servant of the high priest, and cut off his right ear.

But Jesus answered, *"Let me at least do this"*—and he touched his ear, and healed him. Jesus said to the chief priests, captains of the temple, and elders, who had come against him, *"Have you come out as against a robber, with swords and clubs? When I was with you in the temple daily, you didn't stretch out your hands against me. But this is your hour, and the power of darkness."*

They seized him, and led him away, and brought him into the high priest's house. But Peter followed from a distance. When they had kindled a fire in the middle of the courtyard, and had sat down together, Peter sat among them. A certain servant girl saw him as he sat in the light, and looking intently at him, said, "This man also was with him."

He denied Jesus, saying, "Woman, I don't know him."

After a little while someone else saw him, and said, "You also are one of them!"

But Peter answered, "Man, I am not!"

After about one hour passed, another confidently affirmed, saying, "Truly this man also was with him, for he is a Galilean!"

But Peter said, "Man, I don't know what you are talking about!" Immediately, while he was still speaking, a rooster crowed. The Lord turned and looked at Peter. Then Peter remembered the Lord's word, how he said to him, *"Before the rooster crows you will deny me three times."* He went out, and wept bitterly.

The men who held Jesus mocked him and beat him. Having blindfolded him, they struck him on the face and asked him, "Prophesy! Who is the one who struck you?" They spoke many other things against him, insulting him.

As soon as it was day, the assembly of the elders of the people were gathered together, both chief priests and scribes, and they led him away into their council, saying, "If you are the Christ, tell us."

But he said to them, *"If I tell you, you won't believe, and if I ask, you will in no way answer me or let me go. From now on, the Son of Man will be seated at the right hand of the power of God."*

They all said, "Are you then the Son of God?"

He said to them, *"You say it, because I am."*

They said, "Why do we need any more witness? For we ourselves have heard from his own mouth!"

ARCHAEOLOGICAL AND HISTORICAL EVIDENCE:

Historically the Passover holiday has been celebrated by Jewish people throughout their history. It was celebrated for approximately 1500 years before Jesus, and has been celebrated for 2,000 years since Jesus. The Passover meal is conducted in remembrance of God saving the Jewish people from the spirit of death, when God took the first born son of every Egyptian, before the Israelites were freed as slaves in the Exodus.

As it relates to the Passover meal, it's helpful to examine whether the Exodus was a real event. "Although Biblical scholars and archaeologists argue about various aspects of Israel's Exodus from Egypt, many of them agree the Exodus occurred in some form or another. [..] Evidence is presented that generally supports a 13th-century B.C. Exodus during the Ramesside Period, when Egypt's 19th Dynasty ruled" (22.1). "Egyptian artifacts and sites show that the Biblical text does indeed recount accurate memories from the period to which the Exodus is generally assigned" (2.6).

In the historical context, knowing Jesus was Jewish, it is perfectly logical and reasonable that Jesus would celebrate the Passover meal with His disciples. Historically, we also know the Passover meal is symbolic of the pending death of Jesus as the lamb slain for our sins. Passover with Jesus established what is now known as communion, and it is taken in remembrance of Jesus. Therefore, the setting in this chapter with the Passover meal, is perfectly reasonable and logical.

As far as the disciple named Judas Iscariot goes, there is a historical document referencing him. "The Gospel of Judas, a text dated to about A.D. 280, tells the story of Judas as a collaborator with Jesus instead of a betrayer" (22.2). With this early, historical document about Judas, it could be reasonable to assume Judas was a real person who knew Jesus. However, we must carefully distinguish the facts versus fictional content within the document. Because the book was written 250 years after Judas lived, and it wasn't written by Judas, the content is mostly interpretive in nature.

For example, the story of Judas in this late gospel would be about as reliable as our story would be if we wrote a book from the viewpoint of a historical figure from 200 years ago. We've never met the historical person, so any thoughts, motives, and character traits for the person would be creative in nature. Therefore, we have to be cautious about what we take from the Gospel of Judas, since a good portion of it is likely to be fictional. The main question we can ask ourselves is how likely it is that Judas was a real person who knew Jesus, since someone felt compelled to write an account of the events from Judas' point of view.

Another small piece of evidence in favor of Judas being a real person is an ancient graveyard in Jerusalem associated with Judas Iscariot. When Judas betrayed Jesus for 30 silver pieces, the blood money was used to purchase a field for burials. The "Field of Blood" exists in Jerusalem today (22.4).

Regarding the Apostle Peter, we discussed him briefly in chapters 4 and 7. Therefore, I won't cover much additional information about Peter here, other than to mention an external (to the Bible) reference of Peter made in a historical document. "The earliest testimony to the apostle Peter's presence in Rome is a letter from a Christian deacon named Gaius. Writing probably toward the end of the second century A.D.—so, around 170 or 180 A.D.—Gaius tells about the wondrous things in Rome, including something called a tropaion where Peter established a church—in fact, the Church, the Roman Catholic church at the site where St. Peter's Basilica is today" (22.3). This is one of several historical references to the Apostle Peter, which further verifies Peter was a real person who followed Jesus.

This chapter also references Jesus going to the Mount of Olives to pray. As you may recall, we covered the archaeology of the Mount of Olives in chapter 19. The Mount of Olives still exists in the world today, making it a factual reality throughout our history.

WHAT DO YOU THINK?

> Thirty pieces of silver was a lot of money in the era of Jesus. Knowing human nature and criminal acts throughout time, what sinful thoughts and motives could cause Judas to betray Jesus, other than just financial gain? In other words, what sinful motives probably resided in Judas' heart and soul?

> At the Passover supper, Jesus established a new covenant. He symbolically spoke of His body and blood being sacrificed by eating of bread and drinking the wine. In what way(s) was the establishment of communion an effective way to ensure ongoing remembrance of Jesus for us?

➢ Virtually all analysts agree the Gospel of Judas is mostly fictional, but the Gospels of Matthew, Mark, Luke, and John are primarily factual. What kinds of skills or evidence can discerning people use to determine whether ancient writings are factual versus fictional?

___

➢ The Apostle Peter was widely accepted as the first leader of the early church movement and as founder of the Catholic Church. Why do you think Peter is widely accepted as being a real person, but people hesitate to accept Jesus as a real person, even though Peter would never have established the Catholic church if Jesus never existed?

___

➢ When Jesus gave His disciples instructions about preparation for the Passover meal, He spoke of His suffering and Judas' betrayal before it happened. Jesus also told Peter he would deny Jesus three times before Peter did it. Jesus stated exactly what would happen in the future. In what ways do you think Jesus's prophetic abilities show He is not just an ordinary man? From where do you think Jesus got His ability to repeatedly, accurately speak of future events?

___

CHAPTER 23

The whole company of them rose up and brought him before Pilate. They began to accuse him, saying, "We found this man perverting the nation, forbidding paying taxes to Caesar, and saying that he himself is Christ, a king."

Pilate asked him, "Are you the King of the Jews?"

He answered him, *"So you say."*

Pilate said to the chief priests and the multitudes, "I find no basis for a charge against this man."

But they insisted, saying, "He stirs up the people, teaching throughout all Judea, beginning from Galilee even to this place." But when Pilate heard Galilee mentioned, he asked if the man was a Galilean. When he found out that he was in Herod's jurisdiction, he sent him to Herod, who was also in Jerusalem during those days.

Now when Herod saw Jesus, he was exceedingly glad, for he had wanted to see him for a long time, because he had heard many things about him. He hoped to see some miracle done by him. He questioned him with many words, but he gave no answers. The chief priests and the scribes stood, vehemently accusing him.

Herod with his soldiers humiliated him and mocked him. Dressing him in luxurious clothing, they sent him back to Pilate. Herod and Pilate became friends with each other that very day, for before that they were enemies with each other.

Pilate called together the chief priests, the rulers, and the people, and said to them, "You brought this man to me as one that perverts the people, and behold, having examined him before you, I found no basis for a charge against this man concerning those things of which you accuse him. Neither has Herod, for I sent you to him, and see, nothing worthy of death has been done by him. I will therefore chastise him and release him."

Now he had to release one prisoner to them at the feast. But they all cried out together, saying, "Away with this man! Release to us Barabbas!"— one who was thrown into prison for a certain revolt in the city, and for murder.

Then Pilate spoke to them again, wanting to release Jesus, but they shouted, saying, "Crucify! Crucify him!"

He said to them the third time, "Why? What evil has this man done? I have found no capital crime in him. I will therefore chastise him and release him." But they were urgent with loud voices, asking that he might be crucified. Their voices and the voices of the chief priests prevailed. Pilate decreed that what they asked for should be done. He released him who had been thrown into prison for insurrection and murder, for whom they asked, but he delivered Jesus up to their will.

When they led him away, they grabbed Simon of Cyrene, coming from the country, and laid on him the cross, to carry it after Jesus. A great multitude of the people followed him, including women who also mourned and lamented him. But Jesus, turning to them, said, *"Daughters of Jerusalem, don't weep for me, but weep for yourselves and for your children. For behold, the days are coming in which they will say, 'Blessed are the barren, the wombs that never bore, and the breasts that never nursed.' Then they will begin to tell the mountains, 'Fall on us!' and tell the hills, 'Cover us.' For if they do these things in the green tree, what will be done in the dry?"*

There were also others, two criminals, led with him to be put to death. When they came to the place that is called "The Skull", they crucified him there with the criminals, one on the right and the other on the left.

Jesus said, *"Father, forgive them, for they don't know what they are doing."*

Dividing his garments among them, they cast lots. The people stood watching. The rulers with them also scoffed at him, saying, "He saved others. Let him save himself, if this is the Christ of God, his chosen one!"

The soldiers also mocked him, coming to him and offering him vinegar, and saying, "If you are the King of the Jews, save yourself!"

An inscription was also written over him in letters of Greek, Latin, and Hebrew: "THIS IS THE KING OF THE JEWS."

One of the criminals who was hanged insulted him, saying, "If you are the Christ, save yourself and us!"

But the other answered, and rebuking him said, "Don't you even fear God, seeing you are under the same condemnation? And we indeed justly, for we receive the due reward for our deeds, but this man has done nothing wrong." He said to Jesus, "Lord, remember me when you come into your Kingdom."

Jesus said to him, *"Assuredly I tell you, today you will be with me in Paradise."*

It was now about the sixth hour, and darkness came over the whole land until the ninth hour. The sun was darkened, and the veil of the temple was torn in two. Jesus, crying with a loud voice, said, *"Father, into your hands I commit my spirit!"* Having said this, he breathed his last.

When the centurion saw what was done, he glorified God, saying, "Certainly this was a righteous man." All the multitudes that came together to see this, when they saw the things that were done, returned home beating their breasts. All his acquaintances and the women who followed with him from Galilee stood at a distance, watching these things.

Behold, a man named Joseph, who was a member of the council, a good and righteous man (he had not consented to their counsel and deed), from Arimathaea, a city of the Jews, who was also waiting for God's Kingdom: this man went to Pilate, and asked for Jesus' body. He took it down, and wrapped it in a linen cloth, and laid him in a tomb that was cut in stone, where no one had ever been laid. It was the day of the Preparation, and the Sabbath was drawing near. The women, who had come with him out of Galilee, followed after, and saw the tomb, and how his body was laid. They returned and prepared spices and ointments. On the Sabbath they rested according to the commandment.

ARCHAEOLOGICAL AND HISTORICAL EVIDENCE:

Do we have evidence for Pontius Pilate outside the biblical texts? YES! "In 1961, archaeologists discovered a plaque fragment at Caesarea Maritima, an ancient Roman city along the Mediterranean coast of Israel. The plaque was written in Latin and imbedded in a section of steps leading to Caesarea's Amphitheatre. The inscription includes the following: 'Pontius Pilatus, Prefect of Judea, has dedicated to the people of Caesarea a temple in honor of Tiberius'" (23.1).

In 2018, "scientists announced a seal ring excavated in the late 1960s at Herodium, a desert palace just outside of Bethlehem, carried the inscription 'of Pilates.' The inscription on the badly corroded ring was read using advanced photographic techniques. The copper alloy ring was probably not fancy enough to have actually been worn by Pilate. It was more likely worn by someone who was authorized to act on Pilate's authority and who would use the seal to create official communications" (2.2).

Cornelius Tacitus, a well-known first century Roman historian, also mentioned Pontius Pilate in his well-known text: "Christus, from whom the name had its origin, suffered the extreme penalty during the reign of Tiberius at the hands of one of our procurators, Pontius Pilatus…" (23.1). Not only does Tacitus mention Pontius Pilate outside the biblical record, but he mentions him in relation to Jesus Christ (Christus).

We have both archaeological finds and historical documents pointing to Pontius Pilate as a real, living person. In this case, there's also a direct reference to Jesus Christ as a real person.

We mentioned evidence for Herod Antipas briefly in Chapter 1, alongside his father, Herod the Great (23.2). We'll discuss the son, Herod Antipas, more fully in this chapter.

"Antipas, named as one of the tetrarchs after the death of Herod I, is known from coins, the writings of Josephus and an allusion in the writings of Philo" (23.3). "Coins from the reign of Herod Antipas even bear his name and his title of 'tetrarch,' demonstrating the historical nature of this prominent figure and supporting the claims made about him in the Gospel of Luke. In the writings of Josephus, where he is called Antipas, he is also named as the tetrarch of Galilee and named as the one who ordered the execution of John the Baptizer. Philo, although not mentioning him by name, alludes to Herod Antipas in passing as one of the tetrarch sons of king Herod who were in power over various regions of Judaea Province during the time of Pontius Pilate" (23.3). See reference (23.4) for additional information.

"Thus, Herod Antipas is firmly attested as a local ruler of Galilee during the rule of Pilate and his short involvement in the trial of Jesus is perfectly logical" (23.3).

Unexpectedly, there is archaeological evidence for Simon of Cyrene, who carried Jesus's cross! You wouldn't expect a person with minimal role in history to be one for which we have evidence, but we do.

"In 1941, Israeli archaeologists Eleazer Sukenik and Nahman Avigad found the ossuary with ten others in a first-century A.D. tomb. They published the find in a scholarly journal, but the ossuary group sat unnoticed in a storeroom for the next 60 years. However, as author Tom Powers observes, the selection of Greek and Hebrew names used on the ossuaries suggests a family connection with Cyrene, in North Africa. Could the Simon mentioned on this ossuary be the Biblical Simon of Cyrene, who carried Jesus' cross on the road to Calvary?" (23.5).

On the ossuary, "the first line reads SIMONALE. Significantly, the SIMON part is centered horizontally at the top of the chest and is carved in deeper lines than the rest of the inscription, evident even in photographs, clues that the single name Simon, standing alone, was likely the original inscription on this side. [...] After the deeply–incised SIMON, the following three characters, ALE, are usually regarded, and rightly so, as a false start of Alexander. Here, the amateur engraver, besides embarking on an ungrammatical construction, found himself running out of room and so started over below. The following two lines continue in the same very shallow incisions (mostly invisible in photographs) and form a unit, a proper inscription whose meaning is perfectly clear: "Alexander (son) of Simon" (23.6).

"This late Second Temple period burial chest bears the inscription 'Alexander (son) of Simon,' an exact parallel to the individuals named in the New Testament, in Mark 15:21: Simon of Cyrene, the man who carried Jesus' cross, and his son Alexander. In the BAR article, I suggested that the person whose remains were in the ossuary was very likely the son of the Biblical Simon. From further study of the ossuary, I now believe that it may well have held not only the remains of Alexander, but also those of the Biblical figure himself—Simon of Cyrene" (23.6).

In a personal email from Tom Powers, he emphasized the point to me, "the initial 'SIMON' is engraved much more deeply and legibly than the rest, and also is centered on the chest. The point is that 'SIMON' was likely the first inscription there, chronologically, and the rest added later -- evidence that the ossuary ultimately held the remains of both men."

"Probably the most remarkable of the relics preserved in the venerable Basilica di Santa Croce in Gerusalemme, Rome, is the relic of the 'titulus Christi', the alleged Title of the Holy Cross of Our Savior. According to the tradition, it was brought to Rome by the Emperess Helena in 326 AD, after it was discovered, together with the relics of the True Cross and three holy nails, during the construction of the Basilica of the Holy Sepulchre in Jerusalem. Although it is easy to consider it a pious forgery in reference to the Helena-legend, a careful palaeographic evaluation found serious indications that the 'titulus' is indeed from the time of Christ" (23.7).

"None of the consulted experts for Hebrew, Greek and Latin Palaeography found any indication of a mediaeval or late antique forgery. Instead, they all dated it in the timeframe between the 1st and the 3/4th century AD, with a majority of experts preferring and none of them excluding the 1st century. Therefore it is very well possible that the 'Titulus Crucis' is indeed the title of the cross of Our Lord" (23.7). Carbon dating alone leads secular scholars to believe the Titulus Crucis is a forgery, even without any tangible evidence of it being a forgery.

When it comes to Jesus himself, and His burial in a tomb after His crucifixion, there is evidence for that practice too. "The ground, in both Galilee and Jerusalem, has disgorged a few stunners. In 1968, a skeletal heel nailed to a board by an iron spike was found in an ossuary, or bone box, inside a first-century tomb near Jerusalem. The heel, which belonged to a man named Yehochanan, helped settle a long-simmering debate about the plausibility of Gospel accounts of Jesus's tomb burial. Crucifixion was a punishment reserved for the dregs of society, and some experts had scoffed at the idea that Romans would accord anyone so dispatched the dignity of a proper interment. More likely, Jesus's remains, like those of other common criminals, would have been left to rot on the cross or tossed into a ditch, a fate that might have complicated the resurrection narrative. But Yehochanan's heel offered an example of a crucified man from Jesus's day for whom the Romans permitted Jewish burial" (23.8). Thus, allowing Joseph of Arimathea to place Jesus's body in a tomb is likely, since Yehochanan's heel proves such burials were permitted.

As for the tomb owned by Joseph of Arimathea, where Jesus was placed, "The Church of the Holy Sepulchre in Jerusalem, has been traditionally related to the two holiest sites in Christianity. The first site entails the very spot where Jesus of Nazareth was crucified, while the second site encompasses the empty tomb of Jesus where he was buried and resurrected. Pertaining to the burial site, this spot was later covered by a shrine – which according to legend, was built by the Romans, after Helena, the mother of Roman Emperor Constantine the Great (who ruled from circa 306-337 AD), discovered the tomb around the year 327 AD." (23.9).

"Researchers have confirmed that the tomb structure is indeed around 1700-years old, which makes the result more-or-less consistent with the traditional beliefs. Interestingly enough, the dating of the mortar material of the shrine also does confirm how the structure was later expanded upon and refurbished by successive cultures, ranging from the Byzantines (Eastern Romans), Crusaders to even the Franciscan friars." (23.9).

Lastly, let's take a look at the burial cloths Jesus was wrapped in when He was placed in the tomb. As far as artifacts go, the Shroud of Turin is fascinating. The issue of the shroud being considered a forgery by some has been a matter of controversy. Let us examine the shroud in light of the facts:

"Jewish law required that a body had to be wrapped in linen cloth that had not been mixed with wool. The Shroud of Turin is made of linen." It also corresponds precisely with the sizing used by first-century Jews, being exactly two cubits wide and eight cubits long (23.10).

"In 1978, scholar John Jackson got permission to carry out tests to determine what kind of paint may have been used. What he found when he tested pieces of the cloth is that no binding or mixing agents were used in the color. Jackson's truly astounding find was that it was human blood on the shroud. The blood type has been identified as type AB. Furthermore, there are two distinctive types of blood found on the shroud: pre-mortem blood, the kind before a person dies, and post-mortem, which has undergone changes following death." These would be very difficult components to include in the creation of a forgery, especially in the middle ages (23.10).

"The Sudarium of Oviedo is a (similar) piece of cloth kept at Cathedral of San Salvador in Oviedo, Spain. Many believe it was the cloth used to wrap the face of Christ when He was buried. It has reliably been dated to at least the fifth century, and its history for at least a century prior can be accurately traced (23.10). "Not only was the image on the Shroud of Turin made with human blood, but it is of the same blood type – AB – as the blood on the Sudarium of Oviedo. AB blood is the rarest type in the world, so the fact that it is found in both shrouds is not likely to be a coincidence. Additionally, the facial images on both of the coverings match up exactly. The forensic evidence gathered is strong enough to reasonably conclude that both clothes were used on the same body" (23.10).

"To further reiterate the significance of the blood stains on the cloth, researchers have pointed to the fact that they perfectly resemble what is now known about Roman crucifixions." In Roman crucifixions, nails went through the wrists and the heels. "The image on the shroud shows that the nails went through the wrists and the heels. Furthermore, the shroud shows bloodstains consistent with what the New Testament gospels describe as a crown of thorns being placed on Jesus' head. Using a crown of thorns was not known to be a common practice, and it is unlikely that many other crucifixion victims were subjected to it. All of the evidence suggests that the Shroud of Turin could actually be, in fact, the burial shroud of Jesus Christ" (23.10).

We won't ever know if the shroud truly was used to wrap Jesus' body, but the Shroud of Turin is definitely an amazing artifact to consider when it comes to Jesus' death and resurrection.

WHAT DO YOU THINK?

> In what way, if any, does Tacitus's historical reference to Jesus Christ in a historical document along with the artifacts listed in this chapter impact your belief about Jesus being a real person? How does this account affect your perceived accuracy of Luke's historical account?

> Describe your thoughts in reaction to some people's proclamation that the story about Jesus is a great hoax, and people are believing in a fairytale, if they think Jesus is real.

➢ Which piece of evidence in this chapter convinces you the most that Jesus was crucified, died, and was laid to rest in a tomb? What is your reasoning?

_____
_____
_____
_____
_____
_____

➢ What fascinates you the most about the Shroud of Turin and the matching Sudarium of Oviedo?

_____
_____
_____
_____
_____
_____

➢ Why do you think Jesus's followers didn't quit believing in Him when He died? At this point, who do you think Jesus is?

_____
_____
_____
_____
_____
_____

➢ Those who are adamantly against religion, Jesus, and the Bible believe all of the evidence through the centuries is faked, it's all a hoax, and only gullible people believe Jesus is real. On the other hand, many people believe the artifacts and historical documents prove Jesus was a real person. What are your thoughts or beliefs at this point, and what makes you think the way you do?

_____
_____
_____
_____
_____
_____

CHAPTER 24

But on the first day of the week, at early dawn, they and some others came to the tomb, bringing the spices which they had prepared. They found the stone rolled away from the tomb. They entered in, and didn't find the Lord Jesus' body. While they were greatly perplexed about this, behold, two men stood by them in dazzling clothing. Becoming terrified, they bowed their faces down to the earth.

They said to them, "Why do you seek the living among the dead? He isn't here, but is risen. Remember what he told you when he was still in Galilee, saying that the Son of Man must be delivered up into the hands of sinful men and be crucified, and the third day rise again?"

They remembered his words, returned from the tomb, and told all these things to the eleven and to all the rest. Now they were Mary Magdalene, Joanna, and Mary the mother of James. The other women with them told these things to the apostles. These words seemed to them to be nonsense, and they didn't believe them. But Peter got up and ran to the tomb. Stooping and looking in, he saw the strips of linen lying by themselves, and he departed to his home, wondering what had happened.

Behold, two of them were going that very day to a village named Emmaus, which was sixty stadia from Jerusalem. They talked with each other about all of these things which had happened. While they talked and questioned together, Jesus himself came near, and went with them. But their eyes were kept from recognizing him. He said to them, *"What are you talking about as you walk, and are sad?"*

One of them, named Cleopas, answered him, "Are you the only stranger in Jerusalem who doesn't know the things which have happened there in these days?"

He said to them, *"What things?"*

They said to him, "The things concerning Jesus, the Nazarene, who was a prophet mighty in deed and word before God and all the people; and how the chief priests and our rulers delivered him up to be condemned to death, and crucified him. But we were hoping that it was he who would redeem Israel. Yes, and besides all this, it is now the third day since these things happened. Also, certain women of our company amazed us, having arrived early at the tomb; and when they didn't find his body, they came saying that they had also seen a vision of angels, who said that he was alive. Some of us went to the tomb, and found it just like the women had said, but they didn't see him."

He said to them, *"Foolish men, and slow of heart to believe in all that the prophets have spoken! Didn't the Christ have to suffer these things and to enter into his glory?"* Beginning from Moses and from all the prophets, he explained to them in all the Scriptures the things concerning himself. They came near to the village where they were going, and he acted like he would go further.

They urged him, saying, "Stay with us, for it is almost evening, and the day is almost over."

He went in to stay with them. When he had sat down at the table with them, he took the bread and gave thanks. Breaking it, he gave it to them.

Their eyes were opened and they recognized him, then he vanished out of their sight. They said to one another, "Weren't our hearts burning within us, while he spoke to us along the way, and while he opened the Scriptures to us?" They rose up that very hour, returned to Jerusalem, and found the eleven gathered together, and those who were with them, saying, "The Lord is risen indeed, and has appeared to Simon!" They related the things that happened along the way, and how he was recognized by them in the breaking of the bread.

As they said these things, Jesus himself stood among them, and said to them, *"Peace be to you."*

But they were terrified and filled with fear, and supposed that they had seen a spirit.

He said to them, *"Why are you troubled? Why do doubts arise in your hearts? See my hands and my feet, that it is truly me. Touch me and see, for a spirit doesn't have flesh and bones, as you see that I have."* When he had said this, he showed them his hands and his feet.

While they still didn't believe for joy, and wondered, he said to them, *"Do you have anything here to eat?"*

They gave him a piece of a broiled fish and some honeycomb. He took them, and ate in front of them. He said to them, *"This is what I told you, while I was still with you, that all things which are written in the law of Moses, the prophets, and the psalms, concerning me must be fulfilled."*

Then he opened their minds, that they might understand the Scriptures. He said to them, *"Thus it is written, and thus it was necessary for the Christ to suffer and to rise from the dead the third day, and that repentance and remission of sins should be preached in his name to all the nations, beginning at Jerusalem. You are witnesses of these things. Behold, I send out the promise of my Father on you. But wait in the city of Jerusalem until you are clothed with power from on high."*

He led them out as far as Bethany, and he lifted up his hands, and blessed them. While he blessed them, he withdrew from them, and was carried up into heaven.

They worshiped him, and returned to Jerusalem with great joy, and were continually in the temple, praising and blessing God. Amen.

ARCHAEOLOGICAL AND HISTORICAL EVIDENCE:

"Luke 24:13 explicitly states that the distance to Emmaus was sixty stadia, that is, only about seven miles from Jerusalem" (24.1). "The distance Josephus measures between this Emmaus and Jerusalem (about three and a half miles) also fits with Luke's description of the disciples making the journey to Emmaus from Jerusalem and back again on the same day" (24.1).

"The rabbinic description of Motza as merely a 'place,' matches Josephus' characterization of Emmaus as a 'place', both of which are compatible with Luke's reference to Emmaus as a 'village.' Thus, the combined evidence from Luke's Gospel, Josephus and rabbinic literature strongly supports the identification of Luke's Emmaus with Motza-Kalonya" (24.1). Although there is no conclusive evidence of exactly where Emmaus was, there are historical references to the village, which can be linked to an actual historic city.

Other references to people and places mentioned in this chapter have already been covered earlier in this book. We've already explored historical documents and artifacts corresponding to Galilee, Jerusalem, Nazareth, Apostle Peter, etc., so we won't cover them again here.

WHAT DO YOU THINK?

➤ Peter saw strips of linen in the tomb where Jesus had been. In what ways do Jesus's burial cloths being left behind add credibility to the Shroud of Turin as an artifact in the previous chapter?

- What would someone be likely to do with the burial cloths used to wrap Jesus, if they kept them as a memory keepsake of Jesus Christ? If they believed Jesus is the Messiah, what steps would you expect the person to take in order to preserve the shrouds?

- What would be your emotions if you arrived expecting to see Jesus's dead body, but were greeted by a ghostly, dazzling pair of men inside Jesus's tomb?

- If the majority of people on Earth believe there is a God, and they believe God can do anything, why do you think a lot of people don't believe God actually brought Jesus back to life?

➢ What gives Jesus a strong, ongoing influence on the world more than 2,000 years after He lived? Why hasn't Jesus's influence on people's lives ever ended?

_____
_____
_____
_____
_____
_____
_____
_____

➢ Why have people throughout the centuries continually lifted Jesus up as the Son of God, and as the ultimate example of godliness and righteousness, even when people who follow Jesus have been persecuted, rejected by family and friends, and many have been put to death?

_____
_____
_____
_____
_____
_____
_____
_____

BONUS CHAPTER:
CHAPTER 1 ~ ACTS OF THE APOSTLES

The first book I wrote, Theophilus, concerned all that Jesus began both to do and to teach, until the day in which he was received up, after he had given commandment through the Holy Spirit to the apostles whom he had chosen. To these he also showed himself alive after he suffered, by many proofs, appearing to them over a period of forty days, and speaking about God's Kingdom. Being assembled together with them, he commanded them:

"Don't depart from Jerusalem, but wait for the promise of the Father, which you heard from me. For John indeed baptized in water, but you will be baptized in the Holy Spirit not many days from now."

Therefore when they had come together, they asked him, "Lord, are you now restoring the kingdom to Israel?"

He said to them, *"It isn't for you to know times or seasons which the Father has set within his own authority. But you will receive power when the Holy Spirit has come upon you. You will be witnesses to me in Jerusalem, in all Judea and Samaria, and to the uttermost parts of the earth."*

When he had said these things, as they were looking, he was taken up, and a cloud received him out of their sight. While they were looking steadfastly into the sky as he went, behold, two men stood by them in white clothing, who also said, "You men of Galilee, why do you stand looking into the sky? This Jesus, who was received up from you into the sky, will come back in the same way as you saw him going into the sky."

Then they returned to Jerusalem from the mountain called Olivet, which is near Jerusalem, a Sabbath day's journey away. When they had come in, they went up into the upper room where they were staying; that is Peter, John, James, Andrew, Philip, Thomas, Bartholomew, Matthew, James the son of Alphaeus, Simon the Zealot, and Judas the son of James. All these with one accord continued steadfastly in prayer and supplication, along with the women, and Mary the mother of Jesus, and with his brothers.

In these days, Peter stood up in the middle of the disciples (and the number of names was about one hundred twenty), and said, "Brothers, it was necessary that this Scripture should be fulfilled, which the Holy Spirit spoke before by the mouth of David concerning Judas, who was guide to those who took Jesus. For he was counted with us, and received his portion in this ministry. Now this man obtained a field with the reward for his wickedness, and falling headlong, his body burst open, and all his intestines gushed out. It became known to everyone who lived in Jerusalem that in their language that field was called 'Akeldama,' that is, 'The field of blood.' For it is written in the book of Psalms,

'Let his habitation be made desolate.

Let no one dwell in it;' and,

'Let another take his office.'

"Of the men therefore who have accompanied us all the time that the Lord Jesus went in and out among us, beginning from the baptism of John, to the day that he was received up from us, of these one must become a witness with us of his resurrection."

They put forward two, Joseph called Barsabbas, who was also called Justus, and Matthias. They prayed and said, "You, Lord, who know the hearts of all men, show which one of these two you have chosen to take part in this ministry and apostleship from which Judas fell away, that he might go to his own place." They drew lots for them, and the lot fell on Matthias, and he was counted with the eleven apostles.

ARCHAEOLOGICAL AND HISTORICAL EVIDENCE:

I included this bonus chapter from the book of Acts, because it is the beginning of the second book written by Luke. It covers the final events between Jesus and His apostles. The Gospel of Luke primarily covers the span of time during Jesus's life on earth. The book of Acts covers the events with Jesus after His resurrection and the apostles activities during the years following Jesus's departure from earth.

The book of Acts was written with an opening addressed to Theophilus, just like the Book of Luke. I couldn't find any other archaeological evidence or historical documents which reference Theophilus.

Most of the people and places mentioned in this chapter were referenced earlier in this book. I will make note of the chapter in which we covered those topics, so you can review the information, if you would like to.

Judea - see Chapter 1.
Samaria - see Chapter 17.
Peter - see Chapters 4, 7 & 22.
Mary, mother of Jesus - see Chapter 1.

James, brother of Jesus - see Chapter 3.
Judas Iscariot - see Chapter 22.
David - see Chapter 1.
We covered the listed disciples in Chapter 6.

"The eleven surviving apostles chose St. Matthias to replace Judas. It is said that about the year 326, the empress St. Helena found St. Matthias' grave in Jerusalem and sent his relics to the Christians of Trier, Germany. They are still venerated in Trier's Basilica of St. Matthias" (6.1).

While researching to find archaeological evidence and historical documents regarding the list of 12 Apostles in the first chapter of Acts, I found Sean McDowell's Dissertation titled: Historical Evaluation of the Evidence for the Death of the Apostles as Martyrs for Their Faith. It concludes:

"(1) all the apostles were willing to die for their faith, and (2) a number of them actually did experience martyrdom. Their willingness to face persecution and martyrdom indicates more than any other conceivable course their sincere conviction that, after rising from the dead, Jesus indeed appeared to them" (25.1). Sean McDowell's conclusions about the martyrdom of each individual disciple are interesting to read, and he uses a probability scale to rate the likelihood of each disciples' martyrdom.

It is a matter of clear historical record that hundreds of early Christians were killed because they would not stop talking about Jesus, and they refused to recant their testimony. "After Jesus' death, the lives of the disciples were transformed to the point that they endured persecution and even martyrdom. Such strength of conviction indicates that they were not just claiming that Jesus rose from the dead and appeared to them in order to receive some personal benefit. They really believed it. [..] They willingly endangered themselves by publicly proclaiming the risen Christ" (25.4). It is highly unlikely the disciples would willingly die for something they knew was a lie, so we can conclude they believed wholeheartedly that Jesus was resurrected and lives, as they each proclaimed until their deaths.

The National Catholic Register's article, "Where Are the 12 Apostles Now?" (Ref. 6.1) lists the disposition of each of the disciples' bodies. Together with historical documentation, knowing where the bodies of several of the disciples are enshrined points to them being real people who knew Jesus.

We have examined a lot of evidence showing Jesus, people, places, practices and circumstances mentioned in the Bible are real. There is a lot of archaeological evidence and historical documentation which establishes a factual basis for Jesus and his life on Earth. As evidence continues to mount with modern archaeology, we have a growing body of evidence for the factual nature of Jesus and the Bible.

"Archaeological work has unquestionably strengthened confidence in the reliability of the Scriptural record. More than one archaeologist has found his respect for the Bible increased by the experience of excavation in Palestine. Archaeology has in many cases refuted the views of modern critics." – Millar Burrows, Professor of Archaeology, Yale University (25.2).

"Archaeological excavations in the Holy Land have 'tended to support the historical value of the Gospels, at least as sources of information about the conditions of their times'" (25.3).

The fact that so many people wrote about, talked about, and continue to spread the news about Jesus and his resurrection from his death forward, is a solid indicator that Jesus was exceptional and real.

Having the Earth's entire timeline changed from the B.C. (Before Christ) era to the A.D. (Anno Domini) era because of Jesus indicates Jesus forever changed the history of Earth from His birth onward. The people of His era clearly believed Jesus was the Son of God, the Messiah, who was resurrected. The ancient eye-witnesses are the most reliable witnesses to the events that occurred during their lifetimes. Ancient artifacts and documentation speak loudly of the real life of Jesus.

WHAT DO YOU THINK?

> Name any proven, factual evidence you can think of which proves Jesus was not real. What role do you think people's backgrounds play in their belief "Jesus isn't real"?

➢ Why were so many 1st century individuals willing to die, saying Jesus was resurrected and truly is the Son of God, rather than recant their story? What is the most likely reason the first century people believed Jesus is real and that He is the prophesied Messiah?

➢ If the Bible and Jesus are a hoax, why did multitudes of people who actually knew Jesus continue following Jesus after He was crucified, dead, and buried? If Jesus just died and that was the end of Jesus, why hasn't anyone ever been able to prove everything about Jesus is fictional or just a hoax?

➢ Skeptics and atheists think 44 independent, Biblical authors, wrote 66 books over more than 1500 years, and collaboratively created the biggest, ongoing, 'fictional' fairytale hoax of all time, and they believe only gullible people believe in God and the Bible. What would be your response to them?

➤ Conversely, how does the ongoing discovery of verified archaeological and historical evidence increasingly support Jesus as a real man? In what ways does the evidence impact your beliefs about the Bible and Jesus?

_____
_____
_____
_____
_____
_____
_____
_____
_____
_____

➤ Based on what you know, what are your thoughts about Jesus? Who do you say Jesus is?

_____
_____
_____
_____
_____
_____
_____
_____
_____
_____
_____
_____

CONCLUSION

There are some aspects of the Jesus narrative which require faith. For example, Jesus's Miracles, His healings, and His resurrection are all matters of faith rather than provable facts. Therefore, we must consider all historical and archaeological evidence, give consideration to eyewitnesses living in Jesus's era over opinions of people more than 2000 years later, and ask ourselves why people in Jesus' day followed Him. We also need to consider whether we believe God is real and able to do anything.

When it comes to archeological evidence, "It may be stated categorically that no archaeological discovery has ever controverted a biblical reference", and "Scores of archaeological findings have been made which confirm in clear outline or exact detail historical statements in the Bible" (26.1).

Archaeologist William F. Albright observes: "The excessive skepticism shown toward the Bible by important historical schools of the eighteenth-and-nineteenth centuries, certain phases of which still appear periodically, has been progressively discredited. Discovery after discovery has established the accuracy of innumerable details, and has brought increased recognition to the value of the Bible as a source of history" (26.2).

Likewise, Joseph Free confirms: "Archaeology has confirmed countless passages which had been rejected by critics as unhistorical or contrary to known facts" (26.3).

Eric Meyers, an archaeologist and emeritus professor in Judaic studies at Duke University says, "I don't know any mainstream scholar who doubts the historicity of Jesus. The details have been debated for centuries, but no one who is serious doubts that he's a historical figure" (i.1).

We have more supporting documentation for the reality of Jesus than we do for other historical figures like Plato, Homer, and Aristotle. So the real issue becomes a question of why people doubt the reality of Jesus, while believing in other historical figures with less proof of their existence.

Ultimately, the judgment is up to you:

Do you believe Jesus was a charismatic figure that everybody followed for His personality, without any basis of truth to what Jesus said and did?

Or do you believe people followed Jesus because He is a miraculous healer, destroyer of demons, and was actually resurrected after He was crucified, dead, and buried?

Do you believe that Jesus was or wasn't a real, living person?

I'll leave those questions with you, so you can ponder what you believe!

To you, I say, "Congratulations! You've completed this study of the Gospel Book of Luke!" Now that you've met Jesus, studied archaeological evidence and historical documentation, you might wonder, "What's next?"

If you've ever prayed a prayer asking Jesus to be the Lord of your life, and asked him to help you overcome your sins in the past, then your next step is to be baptized and to get to know Jesus personally.

If you don't get to know Jesus personally, then you will be open to being innocently deceived. Romans 16:18 warns us about people who lead others astray saying, "For those who are such don't serve our Lord, Jesus Christ, but their own belly; and by their smooth and flattering speech, they deceive the hearts of the innocent."

Additionally, you can't follow Jesus if you don't develop a close relationship by getting to know Him. Everything Jesus taught is important for your spiritual growth. Therefore, it's critical for you to study everything taught in the Bible, and in the end it WILL make your life easier and more fulfilling.

In Matthew 11:29-30, Jesus says, "Take my yoke upon you, and learn from me, for I am gentle and lowly in heart, and you will find rest for your souls. For my yoke is easy, and my burden is light."

Also, do you remember the teachings Jesus gave about how your faith affects the outcome of your prayers? If you do, then you know it's important for you to have faith in Jesus in order to have effective prayers. The best way to strengthen your faith is to get to know Jesus deeply on a personal level.

Studying Jesus helps build your faith. Having faith in Jesus makes your life less burdensome. Spending time studying Jesus' teachings is well worth every minute for making you and your life better.

You can get to know Jesus well by reading all four of the Gospel books in the New Testament. They are the books titled Matthew, Mark, Luke, and John. Each one will give you different insights into who Jesus is and what He taught.

The four Gospels cover Jesus' actions and teachings in detail. If you liked this book's study format, check out the Journal Bible Studies for the other three Gospels:

- *Who is Jesus?* covers the Gospel of Mark;
- *Is Jesus The Savior?* covers the Gospel of Matthew;
- *Is Jesus God?* covers the Gospel of John.

How will you get to know Jesus better? My recommendation is to dive into a study of the Gospel of Mark next, in the Journal Bible Study titled, "***Who Is Jesus?***" If you've already read the Gospel of Mark, you can find the other journal Bible studies listed at my website: JournalBibleStudy.com.

Whether you study the New testament, the Old Testament, or read your Bible directly, you will find your knowledge and righteousness will continue to grow, as long as you continue studying the Bible! God's Word is living and it will bring you new insights and spiritual growth throughout your life.

When you study Jesus's teachings and God's expectations, prepare to be amazed. God will bless you throughout your journey. May the Lord give you great insights and inspiration, and develop you into a strong, spirited follower of Jesus Christ!

If you haven't already asked Jesus to come into your life as your Savior, it's really easy to do. The next section is for you!

If YOU WANT TO JESUS TO BECOME YOUR SAVIOR:

All you have to do is ask Jesus to be your Lord and Savior. Here's what the Bible says about being saved:

- **Romans 10:9-10** says, "If you will confess with your mouth that Jesus is Lord, and believe in your heart that God raised him from the dead, you will be saved. For with the heart, one believes unto righteousness; and with the mouth confession is made unto salvation."

- **Romans 10:13** says, "Whoever will call on the name of the Lord will be saved." The name of the Lord is Jesus.

- **Mark 16:16** says, "He who believes and is baptized will be saved; but he who disbelieves will be condemned." Here, belief is the main key to being saved, but baptism is an act of faith for those who believe.

To be saved and have Jesus come into your life, it's as easy as believing Jesus is God's Son. With all sincerity, ask Jesus to save you and to become Lord in your life. You can do this easily by praying the following prayer:

"Lord Jesus, I believe you are God's Son, and God resurrected you from the dead. Please come into my life as my Lord and Savior, and save me from my sins. In Jesus' name I pray, Amen."

For a deeper understanding of the concept of being saved, the book of John, Chapter 3:14-21 (quoted below) will help you. Keep in mind, when these verses say 'light,' they mean Jesus, because He is the Light to the world:

"As Moses lifted up the serpent in the wilderness, even so must the Son of Man (Jesus) be lifted up, that whoever believes in Him should not perish, but have eternal life. *For God so loved the world, that He gave His one and only Son (Jesus), that whoever believes in Him should not perish, but have eternal life.* For God didn't send His Son into the world to judge the world, but that the world should be saved through Him (Jesus). The person who believes in Him (Jesus) is not judged. The person who doesn't believe has been judged already, because he has not believed in the name of the one and only Son of God. This is the judgment, that the light (Jesus) has come into the world, and men loved the darkness rather than the light; for their works were evil. For everyone who does evil hates the light, and doesn't come to the light (Jesus), lest his works would be exposed. But he who does the truth comes to the light (Jesus), that his works may be revealed, that they have been done in God."

May God bless you in the days ahead as you seek Jesus, His truth, and light.

Going forward, I pray you are greatly blessed whenever you spend time reading your Bible, praying, and in fellowship with other believers. I pray you will find a church family you love, and you will seek to be baptized, if you haven't been already.

And remember always, if you prayed the prayer asking Jesus to be your Lord because you believe in Him, **you are saved!**

♥ CONGRATULATIONS and May God Bless YOU now and forever! ♥

REFERENCE LINKS

INTRODUCTION

i.1 – Copan, Paul, "Prove to Me That God Exists": Getting Clear on Atheism, Agnosticism, and a Few Other Matters," accessed 8 October 2019 at:
http://www.paulcopan.com/articles/pdf/Atheism_Agnosticism_and_Theism-Copan.pdf

i.2 – The Gospel of Luke, accessed 9 October 2019 at: https://www.blueletterbible.org/study/intros/luke.cfm

CHAPTER 1

1.1 – Jensen, Morten Hørning, Antipas—The Herod Jesus Knew, accessed 9 October 2019 at:
https://www.baslibrary.org/biblical-archaeology-review/38/5/4

1.2 – By Barbara Kreiger, August 2009. Smithsonian Magazine, accessed July 2019 at:
https://www.smithsonianmag.com/history/finding-king-herods-tomb-34296862/

1.3 – Israel Ministry of Foreign Affairs, 08 May 2007. Tomb of King Herod discovered at Herodium, accessed 8 October 2019 at:
https://mfa.gov.il/mfa/israelexperience/history/pages/tomb%20of%20king%20herod%20discovered%2008-may-2007.aspx

1.4 – Klimczak, Natalia. 2 August 2016. Accessed July 2019 at: https://www.ancient-origins.net/ancient-places/empty-tomb-and-site-full-faith-where-was-virgin-mary-buried-006379

1.5 – Tomb of the Blessed Virgin Mary, accessed 9 October 2019 at:
http://www.newadvent.org/cathen/14774a.htm

1.6 – K., Michael, Excavation at Gezer, Accessed July 2019 at:
http://theworldofbiblicalarchaeology.blogspot.com/2011/12/excavation-at-gezer-ancient-calendar.html

1.7 – Gezer Calendar, Accessed July 2019 at: http://www.unamsanctamcatholicam.com/history/biblical-archaeology/97-history/biblical-archaeology/476-gezer-calendar.html

1.8 – https://en.m.wikipedia.org/wiki/Judea, Accessed 2 October 2019, used under CC License as specified at: https://en.wikipedia.org/wiki/Wikipedia:Text_of_Creative_Commons_Attribution-ShareAlike_3.0_Unported_License.

1.9 – Pelgrift, Henry Curtis, 23 September 2015. The Cave of Elijah the Prophet under Threat? A place sacred to Elijah in the Bible, accessed 9 October 2019 at: https://www.biblicalarchaeology.org/daily/news/the-cave-of-elijah-the-prophet-under-threat/

1.10 – Peterson, Daniel, 12 March 2015., Archaeology and the boyhood of Jesus in Nazareth, accessed 9 October 2019: https://www.deseret.com/2015/3/12/20560451/archaeology-and-the-boyhood-of-jesus-in-nazareth

1.11 – Biblical Archaeology Society Staff, 02 May 2019, The Tel Dan Inscription: The First Historical Evidence of King David from the Bible, accessed 9 October 2019 at: https://www.biblicalarchaeology.org/daily/biblical-artifacts/the-tel-dan-inscription-the-first-historical-evidence-of-the-king-david-bible-story/

1.12 – Wood, Dr. Bryant G., Associates for Biblical Research. Is there archaeological evidence of the sons of Jacob, the tribal leaders of Israel? Accessed 2 October 2019 at: https://christiananswers.net/q-abr/abr-a028.html.

1.13 – Astle, Cynthia. 4 May 2019. Archaeological Evidence About the Biblical Story of Abraham, accessed 9 October 2019 at: https://www.learnreligions.com/archaeological-evidence-abraham-bible-4590053.

CHAPTER 2

2.1 – No Author listed. Augustus. Accessed July 2019 at: https://www.romanemperors.com/augustus.htm

2.2 – Govier, Gordon. 27 December 2018. Biblical Archaeology's Top 10 Discoveries of 2018, Accessed 2 October 2019 at: https://www.christianitytoday.com/news/2018/december/biblical-archaeology-top-10-discoveries-2018-israel.html

2.3 – White, Ellen, 18 December 2018, Has the Childhood Home of Jesus Been Found? Jesus' home in Nazareth. Accessed 2 October 2019 at: https://www.biblicalarchaeology.org/daily/biblical-sites-places/biblical-archaeology-sites/has-the-childhood-home-of-jesus-been-found/

2.4 – https://en.wikipedia.org/wiki/Calendar_Inscription_of_Priene, Accessed 2 October 2019, used under CC License as specified at: https://en.wikipedia.org/wiki/Wikipedia:Text_of_Creative_Commons_Attribution-ShareAlike_3.0_Unported_License.

2.5 – Wallace, J. Warner, 15 May, 2017, A Brief Sample of Archaeology Corroborating the Claims of the New Testament: WHAT THE ARCHAEOLOGICAL RECORD SHOWS, accessed 8 October 2019 at: http://www.breakpoint.org/2017/05/brief-sample-archaeology-corroborating-claims-new-testament/

2.6 – Exodus Evidence: An Egyptologist Looks at Biblical History, Biblical Archaeology Review 42:3, May/June 2016. Accessed 2 October 2019 at: https://www.baslibrary.org/biblical-archaeology-review/42/3/2

2.7 – Biblical Archaeology Society Staff, 24 March 2019. The Exodus: Fact or Fiction? Evidence of Israel's Exodus from Egypt, Accessed 2 October 2019 at: https://www.biblicalarchaeology.org/daily/biblical-topics/exodus/exodus-fact-or-fiction/

CHAPTER 3

3.1 – No Author listed. Tiberius. Accessed July 2019 at: https://www.romanemperors.com/tiberius.htm

3.2 – No Author listed. Pontius Pilate, Accessed 2 October 2019 at: https://www.allaboutarchaeology.org/pontius-pilate-faq.htm.

3.3 – No author listed. The Book of Acts—The Church Begins, Accessed 9 October 2019 at: https://www.ucg.ca/booklets/bible-and-archaeology-part-2/book-acts-church-begins

3.4 – Telegraph Reporters, 15 Jun 2012. Scientists find new evidence supporting John the Baptist bones theory, Accessed 9 October 2019 at: https://www.telegraph.co.uk/news/religion/9333052/Scientists-find-new-evidence-supporting-John-the-Baptist-bones-theory.html

3.5 – Biblical Archaeology Org, Herod the Great (Image), Accessed 9 October 2019 at: https://www.biblicalarchaeology.org/wp-content/uploads/2017/09/herodian-family-tree.jpg

3.6 – Shanks, Hershel, 11 November 2013. Israel Antiquities Authority Returns 'Jesus Brother' Bone Box to Owner, Accessed 9 October 2019 at: https://www.biblicalarchaeology.org/daily/news/israel-antiquities-authority-returns-jesus-brother-bone-box-to-owner/

3.7 – https://en.m.wikipedia.org/wiki/Herodian_Tetrarchy, Accessed 2 October 2019, used under CC License as specified at: https://en.wikipedia.org/wiki/Wikipedia:Text_of_Creative_Commons_Attribution-ShareAlike_3.0_Unported_License.

3.8 – Peterson , Daniel, 14 September 2017. Evidence of 23 New Testament political figures outside of the Bible, Accessed 9 October 2019 at: https://www.deseret.com/2017/9/14/20619396/evidence-of-23-new-testament-political-figures-outside-of-the-bible

3.9 – https://www.biblicalarchaeology.org/daily/people-cultures-in-the-bible/people-in-the-bible/new-testament-political-figures-the-evidence/

3.10 – No author listed. Iturea, Accessed 9 October 2019 at: https://www.bible-history.com/geography/ancient-israel/iturea.html

3.11 – No author listed. Trachontis, Accessed 9 October 2019 at: https://www.bible-history.com/geography/ancient-israel/trachonitis.html

3.12 – No author listed. Abilene, Accessed 9 October 2019 at: https://www.bible-history.com/geography/ancient-israel/abilene.html

3.13 – Bohstrom, Philippe, 12 July 2016, Archaeologists Uncover Life of Luxury in 2,000-year-old Priestly Quarters of Jerusalem, accessed October 2019 at: https://www.haaretz.com/whdcMobileSite/archaeology/priestly-quarter-of-ancient-jerusalem-found-on-mt-zion-1.5409239.

3.14 – UNESCO, Baptism Site "Bethany Beyond the Jordan" (Al-Maghtas), Accessed 7 October 2019 at: https://whc.unesco.org/en/list/1446/, Adapted from quotation under CC license at: https://whc.unesco.org/en/licenses/6

CHAPTER 4

4.1 – No author listed. Capernaum, Accessed 2 October 2019 at: https://www.allaboutarchaeology.org/capernaum.htm.

4.2 – No author listed. SIDON, THE CITY, Accessed 9 October 2019 at: http://www.sidonexcavation.com/index.php/2016-01-07-16-38-40/sidon-the-city

4.3 – Unknown Author, "Archaeologists Bring Ancient Zarephath To Life," Bible and Spade Vol 2:1, 1973, p. 23. Accessed 9 October 2019 at: http://www.galaxie.com/article/bsp02-1-06

4.4 – Holloway, April, 28 JULY 2013. Archaeologists may have found home of Bible Prophet Elisha, Accessed 9 October 2019 at: https://www.ancient-origins.net/news-history-archaeology/archaeologists-may-have-found-home-bible-prophet-elisha-00697

4.5 – Lewis, Nicola Denzey, 08 May 2019. The Apostle Peter in Rome: Jesus' chief disciple examined, Accessed 9 October 2019 at: https://www.biblicalarchaeology.org/daily/people-cultures-in-the-bible/people-in-the-bible/the-apostle-peter-in-rome/

CHAPTER 5

5.1 – Garroway, Joshua. Pharisees, Accessed 9 October 2019 at: https://www.bibleodyssey.org/en/people/main-articles/pharisees

5.2 – No Author Listed. The Pharisees – Jewish Leaders in the First Century AD, Accessed 9 October 2019 at: https://www.bible-history.com/pharisees/PHARISEESConclusion.htm

CHAPTER 6

6.1 – Craughwell, Thomas, 28 April 2017. Where Are the 12 Apostles Now? Accessed 2 October 2019 at: http://m.ncregister.com/blog/tcraughwell/where-are-the-12-apostles-now.

6.2 – Emily Jones, 14 August 2019. Archaeologists Find Church of The Apostles Built Over Home of Jesus' Disciples. Accessed 2 October 2019 at: https://www1.cbn.com/cbnnews/israel/2019/august/archaeologists-find-church-of-the-apostles-built-over-home-of-jesus-disciples

6.3 – Biblical Archaeology Society Staff, 06 August 2017. Tomb of Apostle Philip Found: Discovery made at Hierapolis, one of the major Christian sites in Turkey. Accessed 9 October 2019 at: https://www.biblicalarchaeology.org/daily/biblical-sites-places/biblical-archaeology-sites/tomb-of-apostle-philip-found/

6.4 – Argubright, John, Bible Believer's Archaeology, Volume 1: Historical Evidence That Proves the Bible, Accessed at https://books.google.com/books?id=fdxaAQAAQBAJ&pg=PA38&lpg=PA38 on 2 October 2019.

6.5 – UNESCO, Accessed 7 October 2019 at: https://www.researchgate.net/profile/Vanessa_Boschloos/publication/311583768_Belgian_archaeologists_in_Tyre_Lebanon_UNESCO_Heritage_Phoenician_Seals_and_Ancient_Curses/links/5981c1094585150575c038f7/Belgian-archaeologists-in-Tyre-Lebanon-UNESCO-Heritage-Phoenician-Seals-and-Ancient-Curses.pdf, CC license given at: https://whc.unesco.org/en/licenses/6

CHAPTER 7

7.1 – No Author listed. Naim. Accessed 9 October 2019 at: https://biblewalks.com/sites/naim.html

7.2 – No Author listed. Nain. Accessed 9 October 2019 at: https://www.seetheholyland.net/nain/

7.3 – Cartwright, Mark, 04 July 2014. Centurion. Accessed 9 Oct. 2019 at: https://www.ancient.eu/Centurion/

CHAPTER 8

8.1 – Meyers, Eric M., Villages of Galilee. Accessed 9 October 2019 at: http://www.bibleodyssey.org/places/related-articles/villages-of-galilee

8.2 – https://en.m.wikipedia.org/wiki/Gergesa, Accessed 1 October 2019, used under CC License as specified at: https://en.wikipedia.org/wiki/Wikipedia:Text_of_Creative_Commons_Attribution-ShareAlike_3.0_Unported_License.

8.3 – No Author listed. THE NEW TESTAMENT AUTHORS. Accessed 9 October 2019 at: http://godisforus.com/information/bible/ntdocs/authors.htm

8.4 – Warner, J., 30 October 2017. Is There Any Evidence for Jesus Outside the Bible? Accessed 9 October 2019 at: https://coldcasechristianity.com/writings/is-there-any-evidence-for-jesus-outside-the-bible/

8.5 – Broussard, Karlo, 3 September 2018. Did Jesus Raise the Dead? Examining the Evidence. Accessed 9 October 2019 at: https://www.catholic.com/magazine/online-edition/did-jesus-raise-the-dead-examining-the-evidence

8.6 – Miller, Mark. 6 August 2015. Archaeologists Excavate Possible Home of Mary Magdalene and Synagogue Where Jesus May Have Preached. Accessed 9 October 2019 at: https://www.ancient-origins.net/history-archaeology/archaeologists-excavate-possible-home-mary-magdalene-and-synagogue-020472

8.7 – Sutton, Candace, 28 July 2018. How Jesus' female disciples who made Christianity happen were wiped from history. Accessed 9 October 2019 at: https://www.news.com.au/world/middle-east/how-jesus-female-disciples-who-made-christianity-happen-were-wiped-from-history/news-story/b398dbb1e22d44e9b20b2f82ebea9516

CHAPTER 9

9.1 – Bethsaida Excavations Project. Publications. Accessed 9 October 2019 at: https://bethsaidaarchaeology.org/publications/

9.2 – Biblical Archaeology Publications. Jerusalem. Accessed 9 October 2019 at: https://www.biblicalarchaeology.org/category/daily/biblical-sites-places/jerusalem/; No Author Listed. Archaeology in Jerusalem. Accessed 9 October 2019 at: https://mfa.gov.il/mfa/aboutisrael/state/pages/archeology%20in%20jerusalem.aspx; and No Author Listed, 2012. Bulla bearing the name Bethlehem. Accessed 9 October 2019 at: http://m.cityofdavid.org.il/en/archeology/finds/bulla-bearing-name-bethlehem

CHAPTER 10

10.1 – Gathercole, Simon. Geography and the Reliability of the Gospels. Accessed 9 October 2019 at: https://www.bethinking.org/is-the-bible-reliable/Geography-and-the-Reliability-of-the-Gospels; Smith, Henry B. Jr.,15 August 2007. Three Woes! Accessed 9 October 2019 at: https://biblearchaeology.org/research/new-testament-era/2330-three-woes

CHAPTER 11

CHAPTER 12

12.1 – Tazpit Press Service. 23 July 2018. Archaeological Sifting Project Confirms Biblical Account of Solomon and David. Accessed 9 October 2019 at: https://www.breakingisraelnews.com/111192/archaeological-sifting-project-confirms-biblical-account-of-solomon-and-david/

CHAPTER 13

13.1 – Buchanan, George Wesley, November 2003. The Tower of Siloam. The Expository Times, http://www.continuumjournals.com/journals/index.asp?jref=24, Vol. 115 No. 2 (November 2003): 37-45. Accessed 9 October 2019 at: http://askelm.com/temple/t031205.htm

CHAPTER 14

CHAPTER 15

CHAPTER 16

CHAPTER 17

17.1 – Katz, Jill, Biblical Archaeology Review 40:3, May/June 2014. Archaeological Views: Jerusalem and Samaria: An Anthropological Tale of Two Cities. Accessed 9 October 2019 at: https://www.baslibrary.org/biblical-archaeology-review/40/3/12 and
Ngo, Robin, 08 March 2018. Ancient Samaria and Jerusalem. Accessed 9 October 2019 at: https://www.biblicalarchaeology.org/daily/archaeology-today/biblical-archaeology-topics/ancient-samaria-and-jerusalem/

CHAPTER 18

18.1 – Ramos, Art, 19 September 2016. Early Jericho. Accessed 9 October 2019 at: https://www.ancient.eu/article/951/

18.2 – No Author listed. Jericho. Accessed 2 October 2019 at: https://www.allaboutarchaeology.org/jericho-archaeology.htm.

CHAPTER 19

19.0 – No Author listed. Zacchaeus Sycamore Tree Jericho. Accessed 9 October 2019 at: https://www.beinharimtours.com/zacheus-sycamore/

19.1 – Kasten, Patricia, 15 April 2016. When taxes came due in Jesus' time. The Compass, Accessed 9 October 2019 at: https://www.thecompassnews.org/2016/04/taxes-came-due-jesus-time/

19.2 – https://en.m.wikipedia.org/wiki/Bethany, Accessed 2 October 2019, used under CC License as specified at: https://en.wikipedia.org/wiki/Wikipedia:Text_of_Creative_Commons_Attribution-ShareAlike_3.0_Unported_License.

19.3 – Mare, W. Harold, 2002, The Archaeology of the Jerusalem Area, on books.google.com, Accessed 8 July 2019 at: https://books.google.com/books?id=QcxKAwAAQBAJ.

19.4 – Kennedy, Titus, 5 March 2018. The Village of Bethphage. Accessed 2 October 2019 at: https://drivethruhistoryadventures.com/the-village-of-bethphage/

19.5 – https://en.m.wikipedia.org/wiki/Mount_of_Olives, Accessed 2 October 2019, used under CC License as specified at: https://en.wikipedia.org/wiki/Wikipedia:Text_of_Creative_Commons_Attribution-ShareAlike_3.0_Unported_License.

CHAPTER 20

20.1 – Sabar, Ariel, January 2016. Unearthing the World of Jesus. Smithsonian Magazine, Accessed 2 October 2019 at: https://www.smithsonianmag.com/history/unearthing-world-jesus-180957515/

20.2 – Cartwright, Mark. "Roman Coinage." Ancient History Encyclopedia. Ancient History Encyclopedia, 19 Apr 2018, Accessed at: https://www.ancient.eu/Roman_Coinage/ 04 Oct 2019.

20.3 – Satlow, Michael L., *Who Were the Sadducees?*, n.p. [cited 4 October 2019]. Online: http://www.bibleodyssey.org/people/related-articles/sadducees.aspx

CHAPTER 21

21.1 – Cartwright, Mark. "Roman Coinage." Ancient History Encyclopedia. Ancient History Encyclopedia, 19 Apr 2018, Accessed 04 Oct 2019 at: https://www.ancient.eu/Roman_Coinage/.

CHAPTER 22

22.1 – Biblical Archaeology Society Staff, 24 March 2019. The Exodus: Fact or Fiction? Evidence of Israel's Exodus from Egypt. Accessed 04 Oct 2019 at: https://www.biblicalarchaeology.org/daily/biblical-topics/exodus/exodus-fact-or-fiction/

22.2 – Pappas, Stephanie, April 08, 2013, Truth Behind Gospel of Judas Revealed in Ancient Inks. Accessed 4 October 2019 at: https://www.livescience.com/28506-gospel-judas-ink-authenticity.html

22.3 – Lewis, Nicola Denzey, May 08, 2019. The Apostle Peter in Rome: Jesus' chief disciple examined. Accessed 10 Oct 2019 at: https://www.biblicalarchaeology.org/daily/people-cultures-in-the-bible/people-in-the-bible/the-apostle-peter-in-rome/

22.4 – Borschel-Dan, Amanda, 4 May 2018, Attempted antiquities looting at site linked to blood money of Judas Iscariot, accessed 8 October 2019 at: https://www.timesofisrael.com/attempted-antiquities-looting-at-site-linked-to-blood-money-of-judas-iscariot/

CHAPTER 23

23.1 – No Author listed. Pontius Pilate. Accessed September 2019 at: https://www.allaboutarchaeology.org/pontius-pilate-faq.htm, Accessed 2 October 2019.

23.2 – Biblical Archaeology Society Staff, June 03, 2017. Herod Antipas in the Bible and Beyond: The ruler of Galilee in Jesus' time. Accessed September 2019 at: https://www.biblicalarchaeology.org/daily/people-cultures-in-the-bible/people-in-the-bible/herod-antipas-in-the-bible-and-beyond/

23.3 – Kennedy, Titus, 02 Sep 2015. The Archaeology of a Trial. Accessed September 2019 at: https://www.hopechannel.com/au/read/the-archaeology-of-a-trial

23.4 – No Author listed. Archaeology and Pontius Pilate. Accessed September 2019 at: https://www.bible-history.com/pontius_pilate/pilateArchaeology.htm

23.5 – Powers, Tom, 2002-2010. A 'Simon of Cyrene' in Jerusalem: The story of the 'Alexander (son) of Simon' ossuary. Accessed September 2019 at: https://israelpalestineguide.files.wordpress.com/2010/06/alexander-son-of-simon-ossuary-illustrated-2010-edit.pdf

23.6 – Powers, Tom, 26 September 2006. A Second Look at the "Alexander Son of Simon" Ossuary: Did It Hold Father and Son? Accessed September 2019 at: https://israelpalestineguide.files.wordpress.com/2010/06/alexander-simon-ossuary-a-second-look-from-bar.pdf

23.7 – Hesemann, Michael, N.D. Titulus Crucis - The title of the cross of Jesus Christ? Accessed September 2019 at: http://michaelhesemann.info/15_8.html

23.8 – By Ariel Sabar, January 2016. Unearthing the World of Jesus. Smithsonian Magazine, Accessed September 2019 at: https://www.smithsonianmag.com/history/unearthing-world-jesus-180957515/

23.9 – Mandal, Dattatreya, 29 Nov 2017, The 'Tomb Of Jesus' Is Around 1,700 Years Old According To Latest Scientific Tests. Accessed September 2019 at: https://www.realmofhistory.com/2017/11/29/tomb-of-jesus-1700-years-old/

23.10 – Trista, N.D. These 16 Facts Reveal Whether the Shroud of Turin Really Belonged to Jesus Christ. Accessed September 2019 at: https://historycollection.co/these-16-facts-reveal-whether-the-shroud-of-turin-really-belonged-to-jesus-christ/7/

CHAPTER 24

24.1 – Bivin, David N., 13 January 2017. A Farewell to the Emmaus Road. Accessed September 2019 at: https://www.jerusalemperspective.com/16208/

CHAPTER 25

25.1 – McDowell, Sean Joslin, December 2014. A Historical Evaluation of the Evidence for the Death of the Apostles as Martyrs for Their Faith. Dissertation, pp 427-428, p. 467, Accessed September 2019 at: https://digital.library.sbts.edu/bitstream/handle/10392/4857/McDowell_sbts_0207D_10221.pdf

25.2 – Burrows, Millar, *What Mean These Stones?* (New York: Meridian Books, 1956), p.1., article cited by Williams, Peter S. Accessed September 2019 at: https://www.bethinking.org/is-the-bible-reliable/archaeology-and-the-historical-reliability-of-the-new-testament

25.3 – Allen, Charlotte, *The Human Christ: The Search for the Historical Jesus* (Oxford: Lion, 1998), p.286., article cited by Williams, Peter S. Accessed September 2019 at: at: https://www.bethinking.org/is-the-bible-reliable/archaeology-and-the-historical-reliability-of-the-new-testament

25. 4 – Habermas, Gary R., Licona, Michael R., The Case for the Resurrection of Jesus. Kregel Publications. p. 56, Accessed 30 October 2019 at: https://books.google.com/books?id-NdF97o5L768C&pg=PA56

CONCLUSION

26.1 – Glueck, Nelson, *Rivers in the Desert: A History of the Negev* (New York: Farrar, Strauss & Cudahy, 1959), p.31., article cited by Williams, Peter S. Accessed September 2019 at: https://www.bethinking.org/is-the-bible-reliable/archaeology-and-the-historical-reliability-of-the-new-testament

26.2 – Albright, William F., The Archaeology of Palestine, pp.127-128, quoted by Josh McDowell, The New Evidence That Demands A Verdict (Nashvile: Thomas Nelson, 1999), p.61., Quoted from article, Does Archaeology Confirm the New Testament?, Accessed September 2019 at: http://www.uncover.org.uk/questions/does-archaeology-confirm-the-new-testament/

26.3 – Free, Joseph, Archaeology and Bible History (Scripture Press, 1969), p.1., Quoted from article, Does Archaeology Confirm the New Testament?, Accessed September 2019 at: http://www.uncover.org.uk/questions/does-archaeology-confirm-the-new-testament/

ABOUT THE AUTHOR

Sandra K. Cook (a.k.a. Sandy) became a Christian when a door-to-door evangelism came to tell her about Jesus. She was saved on the front doorstep of her home when she was in the 10th grade and she asked Jesus to become Lord of her life.

Sandy's life changed dramatically throughout the years that followed. She is refined by fiery trials. Sandy was married at 19, widowed at the age of 22, lived in poverty, was assaulted, and in a bank robbery with a gun held to her head. She was suicidal, struggled mightily with her self-esteem, and felt her life was pointless.

At the time of her first husband's death, Sandy began to read her Bible from cover-to-cover, deeply desiring to understand the purpose of life and to learn about God. Reading the Bible set Sandy's heart on walking with the Lord. She was gripped by the love God proclaims for each one of us, because she often felt unloved and unlovable.

In her life today, Sandy focuses on godly love, above all things, and seeks to help other Christians feel and understand God's love, and to grow their fruit of the spirit. She believes everybody is more than just somebody... Everybody is God's Beloved Child, including YOU, my dear one!

The greatest joys in Sandy's life are spending time with her husband, sons, family, and her friends. Sandy loves reading to learn, studying the Bible, photography, and singing praise songs (although, you do not want to hear her tone deaf singing!)

Sandy earned her Degree of Divinity from the Christian Leaders Institute. She is a certified Biblical Life Coach, has a Master's Degree in Instructional Design, and is a life-long learner.

Sandy prays God will richly bless YOU in your life each and every day! ♥

OTHER BOOKS BY SANDY K. COOK

WHO IS JESUS?

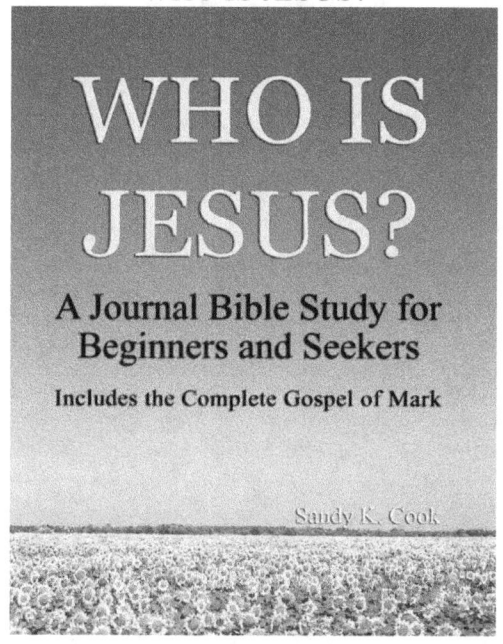

IS JESUS THE SAVIOR?

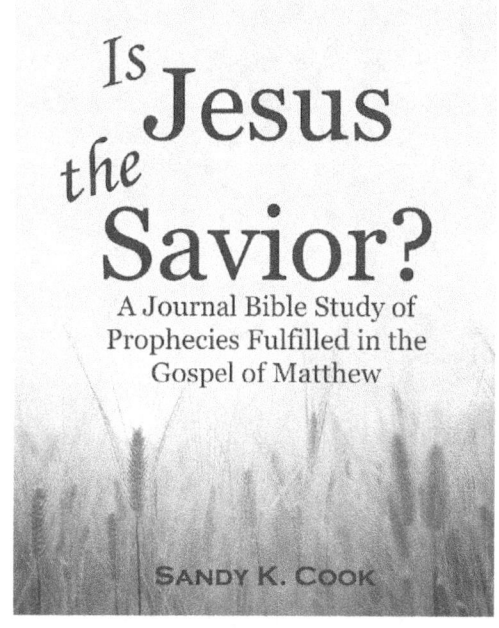

IS JESUS GOD?

BE A PERSON AFTER GOD'S OWN HEART

www.ingramcontent.com/pod-product-compliance
Lightning Source LLC
Chambersburg PA
CBHW081744100526
44592CB00015B/2288